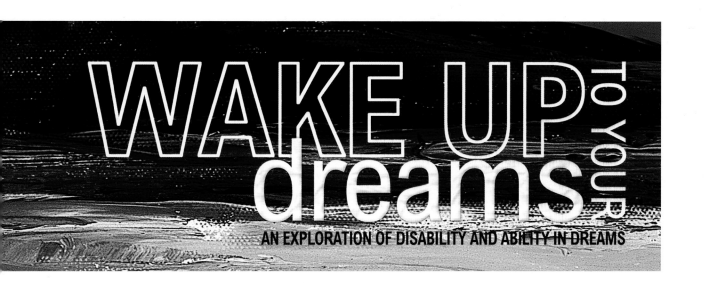

WAKE UP TO YOUR dreams

AN EXPLORATION OF DISABILITY AND ABILITY IN DREAMS

Jean C. Morrison

with illustrations by John Lowrie Morrison

Scottish Christian Press

First published in Great Britain
In 2005 by Scottish Christian Press
21 Young Street
Edinburgh EH2 4HU

ISBN 1904325319

Cover and book layout by Heather Macpherson

Printed and bound by Bookchase Ltd

This book is produced with the aid of a grant from the Board of Parish Education of the Church of Scotland

DEDICATION

To my dear friend Sandi Joy

who has shared with me

over so many years and so freely

her experience of life

as a loving, determined and very able person

ACKNOWLEDGEMENTS

I'm grateful to the following people for their contributions, support and encouragement in the preparation of this book and in my work: thank you.

To John Lowrie Morrison, a long-standing friend, whose skill, sensitivity and generosity in illustrating some dreams in this book has brought words to life - a very big thank you!

To the Board, staff and counsellors, past and present, of the Lothian Centre for Integrated Living, Edinburgh who allowed me to use their agency as my initial research base, and gave me such guidance and encouragement throughout that time.

To all the people who gave me their dream experiences and allowed me to listen, to ask questions, and finally to pass on to others in this book what I learned from them.

To all who challenged and supported me through my research-based learning - especially Dr. John Bomford, Professor Michael Carroll, Drs. Archie Mills, Mark Solms, and Anne Tait; my fellow students and staff at Metanoia Institute, my dear sister-in-law Jill Grigor and my loving, encouraging and patient husband, Bill.

To my friends Dorothy Murray and Barry Wise who, twelve thousand miles apart, read through drafts of my manuscript and gave such helpful feedback, Meg McCallum who scanned chapters where I wanted to check my use of language, and Kay McIntosh who walked with me along windy beaches tossing ideas between us. I owe you a tremendous debt.

Lastly to my many other friends, especially those in the counselling world and the diaconate - thanks for your inspiration and support.

CONTENTS

FOREWORD

Thanks to disability

Over the past few decades, our society has begun radically to change the way we talk about both disability and the lives of disabled people. I have journeyed from a response of irritation at those changes, because they demanded that I stop and think what might lie behind them, to a place where my intention is to think differently and express this by using positive language. I now understand that this use of language carries a new attitude of respect, a new balance of power: one of equality in society. If this feels new to you, consider the difference in attitude implied by the old term 'wheelchair-bound' and the current one 'wheelchair user'.

While working with people in the Lothian Centre for Integrated Living I was given a course in what was then called 'Disability Awareness', and is now better known as 'Disability Equality Training'. I was introduced to various models of thinking and talking about disability - in particular to 'The Medical Model' and 'The Social Model'[1] - and shown how each of these uses language differently. Very briefly, the Medical Model concentrates on what 'goes wrong' with the body and how to help it function more usefully. This conveys the impression that people's lives are disabled by their impaired bodies. The Social Model takes a different viewpoint. It says that society disables people by not making buildings and transport accessible; by labelling people in terms of what they cannot do; by not examining false or outdated assumptions held about the lives of disabled people; by pitying, patronising attitudes.

The focus for much of the research I carried out was on body image in dreams, and on how this differed from body image in waking experience. I had to communicate the difference to readers. In using words to describe in particular the body image of many

[1] Barnes et al (Eds.) reprint 2000

disabled people, and how that differed in their dreams, I landed in what sometimes felt like the chaos of the best practice debate on the correct use of language. If I have given hurt to anyone in my use of language, I apologise. My intention is to challenge (but not through giving offence).

Recently I have become aware of another model - 'The Affirmative Model'[2] - designed by disabled people to express the positive way they think of disability. One of the many aspects this model highlights is the benefit to society that people being impaired and disabled can bring. I would love to think that my research demonstrates this.

The inspiration for this book was an occasion when quite by chance, I participated in a conversation amongst wheelchair users of their experience of walking and dancing in their dreams (this story will be related in more detail in the Introduction). If I had not heard that conversation, it would not have occurred to me to study self-representation in dreams. That was something I had assumed to be unremarkable in my work with non-disabled counselling clients. There appeared to be such a contrast between the dreaming experience of disabled people and that of non-disabled dreamers that I literally sat up and took notice of it (and later discovered that many others had done so before me).

Because disabled people risked sharing their dreams with me so freely, I was motivated to continue studying and to discover that there had been recent and relevant scientific research on the dreaming brain. Other writers had made assumptions on this subject prior to the publication of that research, and had concluded that there were reasons for the dreams of disabled people to be different. Informed by the new research, I could reach a significant new conclusion.

If this book enables anyone better to understand their dreams, it will be a benefit directly attributable to the experience of disabled people.

[2] Swain et al (Eds.), 2003

INTRODUCTION

To introduce this book, I'd like to tell you a bit about myself.

I come from a family of teachers, and in childhood developed the habit of learning, then passing on what I learned to others. What I've been learning over the past five years or so has been a real source of stimulation and inspiration for me, and I want to share it with you. But first, a bit more background.

For many years now I've been in the counselling profession, using developed skills to enable people to learn more about themselves and their relationships. Twenty years ago I was in the position to begin to train others to become counsellors, and after doing that for some years, was invited in 1997 to be one of the trainers in the Lothian Centre for Integrated Living (LCIL) in Edinburgh. Part of LCIL's work is to run a peer counselling service where disabled adults counsel other disabled adults. I responded eagerly to this challenge, and was soon passing on what I had learned elsewhere to some of the counsellors-in-

training, enabling them to reflect on their lives and counselling practice.

It was the summer term of 1998, and a warm day. The lunch break chat ranged over many topics, and as trainer of the group it was time for me to relax. Personal assistants were on hand to meet any physical needs of the group and I was only half listening to the conversation flowing around the room.

I don't recall quite how the topic arose, but I heard one woman from her wheelchair casually announce, 'In my dreams I walk and sometimes I run!' The group's response was immediate: 'me too!' 'I sometimes dance in mine.' 'So can I!' 'I remember climbing a mountain!' All the wheelchair users in the group agreed. I felt astonished! Why should this be? Immediately I felt totally re-engaged with what was going on. I watched their eager expressions as trainees compared notes and realised that something each had thought to be a personal and private experience was a shared one.

Eventually I broke in with 'This sounds wonderful for you!' To my consternation that comment was severely challenged by two women who demanded that I examine my assumption. 'Well,' I said, thinking quickly, 'I remember having dreams where I could fly, and I loved that experience of freedom. I thought it would be the same for you.'

Back came the response, 'But when we waken we can't just jump out of bed and walk.'

That lunchtime conversation was to haunt me. Not for months had I been so conscious that I was a trainer imported into a culture where I felt I did not rightfully belong! I regularly took for granted that I could jump out of bed and walk. On the spur of the moment, and by myself if I so chose, I could go wherever I pleased. Life rarely presented me with a disabling experience. What did I know and understand of their experience of disability? Very little. Some years ago I lost my sense of smell. Potentially this could be a life-threatening problem if there were a gas leak or a fire and I was unaware of it, and it is a nuisance when I forget that a saucepan might boil dry, but in practice this sensory impairment has not affected me professionally. For some years I have had some hearing loss and find it impossible to understand some softly spoken voices, but a hearing aid helps me in most situations, so I experience myself as having an impediment but not as disabled by it. I realise that this makes me part of a large section of the population of over-sixties who have some form of impairment but who have not yet have assumed the identity of being disabled persons. Each adult in that group had some experience of life that directly contrasted with mine, although much of our life experience was shared. Most had been in employment - as teacher, nurse, care assistant, joiner, tree surgeon, hairdresser - and had had to leave it. Each was now in receipt of some form of Disability Allowance; I was self-employed.

All had been accepted on to this counselling course because they wanted to become professionally trained volunteers in helping others like themselves cope more creatively with their lives - I could identify with that.

I had experience of counselling disabled people, but could not recall anyone sharing a dream with me in the process. I had certainly helped non-disabled clients look at their dreams over the years, but if I now had a client with mobility impairment, how would I understand the dream significance of his or her climbing a mountain unaided?

If a non-disabled client had shared with me a dream in which she/ he was climbing a mountain, I would have assumed that the mountain was something symbolic, probably a challenge she was facing in her life. I wouldn't have felt surprised that she was able to climb because I would have taken her mobility for granted. But now, not one, but five disabled people had talked about moving freely in their dreams. I could not take their mobility for granted in day-by-day waking life. I had learned through hard experience, and in discussion with each of them, how to adapt my teaching methods to enable their learning, and not to be a part of the society that thoughtlessly disables them, so my immediate response was not to take their mobility for granted in their dreaming. Why, I wondered, were wheelchair users not in wheelchairs in their dreams, as in their everyday waking experience? Was this not part of their body image and identity?

I was confronted with the need to learn about this dreaming phenomenon, and with it came the energy I needed to devote to this pursuit. After all, I was being trusted and paid to train disabled people to be good counsellors of other disabled people! I needed to know about this particular phenomenon for my own counselling practice, but even more pressing was my need to learn about it so that I could be a good enough trainer in LCIL. If I did not, I would become a disabling factor in their becoming equipped to counsel disabled clients.

It so happened that at that time I had registered on a course of research-based learning so that I could become a doctor of psychotherapy through professional studies. I had to find a topic to begin my research, and decided to start with this.

I had no idea then that it would take me so long to find a satisfactory answer. I discovered that many others before me had asked the same questions, and come to various conclusions, many of which I wanted to refute.

Dreams are powerful stories! The part of my research that involved hearing the dreams of many people with whom I had some relationship, whether formal or informal, was sometimes very challenging both for me and for them. We had to work at maintaining the necessary boundaries, and being in a formal research programme enabled me to do this. I had to learn to balance my need to enquire, discover, and maintain good faith with all who shared their dreams with me, observing their need for privacy and respect.

In the course of trying to discover why disabled people usually dream with a self-representation of a whole and fully functioning body, I learned many other factors, not only about this phenomenon, but also about all dreaming, that I longed to pass on.

I began my research into what I believed to be a phenomenon only seen in the dreams of disabled people, and they contributed many of the examples in this book. What I discovered applies to dreaming in general, although I hope this book will be of particular interest to disabled people themselves.

- Many people from time to time have a dream they long to understand better. There is no quick fix for this, so this is a book written to help any dreamer build up the knowledge and skill to begin interpreting their own dreams.

- Becoming competent in understanding their own dreams should give any reader what she or he needs to help another person begin to understand their dreams.

- I want all dreamers to know that the dreams of disabled people are in no way essentially different from the dreams of non-disabled people: all dreamers from time to time experience their dream-body as differently-abled from their waking body, and the dreams of all dreamers contain symbols from their day-by-day lives.

- I want to let disabled people know why in their dreams they usually have a non-disabled self-image.

- When disabled people share their dreams, I want those who listen not to be too astonished to be helpful.

So, if you are curious about your dreams, come with me as I retrace my journey to understand one dreaming phenomenon. This might help you, as it did me, to wake up to what your dreams hold for you.

1 A JOURNEY OF DISCOVERY

Is the experience of a few disabled people of being fully mobile in their dreams similar for other disabled people, and does something similar apply for those with sensory impairment? (My study focused on the self-image people experienced in their dreams.)

Does this phenomenon exist?

I had heard something that surprised me in the dream life of five wheelchair users. Somehow, I had assumed that the image they would see of themselves in their dreams would be similar to the image they would see if they were passing a large store window, or on film. Surely the kind of image of myself I saw in my dreams was very similar to my photographic image? What might make this so very different for disabled people?

I could not generalise from five examples! First I had to find out if other disabled people had a similar experience, of having a different body image in their dreams from their waking life. Of course, the term 'disability'[3] covers many different experiences, and not all impairment would immediately be apparent in a person's

waking body image. (Some people have hidden impairment only apparent to other people from time to time and in certain circumstances).

What if the dreamer was a person with sensory impairment: if he or she in waking life were unable to see or to hear, to taste or to smell? What if they could no longer speak? Would they have these senses in their dreams? Would there be any difference in dreams between congenitally disabled people and those who had acquired disability in childhood, or later, in adult life?

Some people with mobility or sensory impairment experience very stable physical conditions for much of their life, while others have to manage on-going degenerative conditions in their senses, in muscle tone or bone density, or increasing pain. The process

[3] See 'Foreword'

of growing older usually brings with it conditions springing from natural wear and tear on limbs and organs - increasing frailty or pain that affects mobility and the full functioning of the senses.

Was I about to examine a universal phenomenon in all people with impairment that could be seen or heard by others - that in their dreams all had a dream self with a body and senses able to respond within each dream scenario?

What about the dreams of non-disabled people? Did they always have a fully functioning body in their dreams that behaved exactly as in their waking life?

Consciousness of the self in dreams of all dreamers

Of course, there are many different kinds of dream experience and not all include an awareness of the dreamer having a body.

No embodied self in dreams

In some dreams there is no body image of a person that can be identified as 'that's me'. You are dreaming the dream, but the dream does not include you: it's entirely about other people or things, if indeed there are any people in it at all.

Sometimes it's rather like watching a film made by a stranger. In one of my dreams all I saw was a clock, with something happening to its hands. One of my friends has a recurrent dream where he can see only patterns and shapes. These dreams can be very significant for the dreamer, but the dreamer's body is not part of the dream experience.

Dream self in the audience

At other times, the experience of dreaming is like watching a film where you are one of the main actors: you can see and/or hear your 'dream self' doing things, relating to other people, being in various scenes. Sometimes you just know that a certain character you are watching is yourself, although that dream self may be a different age, gender, of a different ethnic origin or be wearing clothes that don't belong to you. That observed 'self' may well be doing something you would not normally do in your waking life, but yet you know it is you!

Self in the action

In other dreams you are totally involved: right in the middle of the action, just as when you are awake, you don't see your whole body. If you are walking or swimming, fighting or hugging you can often remember when you wake up how these body movements felt as you made them. You may clearly remember thoughts and emotions your dream body experienced, and your reasons for the choices and decisions you made as the dream progressed, even if they don't seem reasonable when you waken! You have been inside your body, completely caught up in that dream world.

I had to find people willing to share their dreams with me, fully aware that I would record and then study what they gave me and eventually write up my findings for others to read.

The participants

It was impossible for me to be in touch with disabled people who represented every kind of impairment. I limited my research to hearing the dreams of people with whom I already had contact, or to whom others referred me and with whom I could communicate personally and easily face to face, by phone or through email.

The age range of men and women who discussed their dreams with me was between mid-twenties and mid-sixties. Some were in full-time employment; some, because of being disabled, had been through the experience of having to leave the job they were trained to do, and some were retraining in other fields; all were people actively interested in other people, many giving services in a voluntary capacity.

Because I worked regularly with thirteen disabled people all involved in training or being trained to become counsellors, I began with them. I was setting out on this journey at least partly so they might understand the meaning of their dreams and could become better equipped to work with the dreams of others in their counselling practice. To my delight the Board of Directors in the Lothian Centre for Integrated Living where I worked part-time, considered a formal application I made to them, granted me permission to begin this research there, and each person I approached within it was willing to participate.

An outline of the research process

The agreement I had with each of the counselling trainees plus a member of staff was that, for a period of six weeks, if he or she had a dream they were willing to share with me for research purposes, they should phone me as soon as possible after having and recording it. When they phoned, we would arrange a mutually convenient time for me to call (as soon as possible) so we could discuss the dream together. Having phoned back I would listen to their dream record, then for about half an hour, help the dreamer explore what he or she thought their dream meant for them. I would facilitate this process by asking questions. I asked specific questions about their dreaming self, and because of what I heard I soon began to add questions about symbols in their dreams that seemed to have some connection with their impairment. Our telephone conversations were recorded, and I would later transcribe them. (I also asked each by which fictitious name they would like to be known when I wrote up my findings).

In my request to the Board I included an outline of the process I would use to explore with the dreamers the meaning of those dreams, included here in an abbreviated version.

I would propose to:

1 Ask the counsellor offering me a dream to tell me the story of their dream

2 Follow that by asking what they thought the dream might be saying to them

3 Ask a further series of questions including:

   - What do you think is the theme of this dream?

   - Which emotions did it stir in you?

   - Have you any thoughts about why you have dreamed this dream now?

4 Since the dream will contain symbolic material I will explore with them what their dream symbols mean for them

5 If the dream contains other persons, I will treat these also as dream symbols

6 I will not attempt to interpret their dreams for them

7 I will remain open to the fact that I might not be able to help a particular person find meaning in a particular dream

This project produced a total of 35 dream records from nine women and four men. Two of those dreamers had been blinded in adulthood, two had hidden disabilities (one with epilepsy), two had mobility impairment from birth, one had had a leg amputated, three had multiple sclerosis, one had Frederick's Ataxia, and two had mobility impairment as a result of accidental injury in adulthood. Eight were wheelchair users, but two of these regularly walked with elbow crutches and kept their wheelchairs only for travelling longer distances.

The first set of results

All 13 dreamers described at least one dream in which their bodies were physically intact and able to go where necessary with their senses functioning well. This was so for 31 out of that total of 35 dreams.

The exceptions were:

- in one of her dreams a woman who is not able to stand for any length of time unaided was standing freely, but in that dream she had no face, although in waking life she has a very lively expressive one

- a man said he was getting around without his chair but not physically walking or moving his limbs, and in this dream he described himself as Tibetan or Chinese

- in two similar dreams in a series one dreamer found herself in her chair heading towards a toilet for disabled people. When the door opened she was in a lift, not a toilet, trapped there while it plummeted towards the ground.

Then there were those where the dream-body began with no sign of impairment, but after a while, floated in the air, or became trapped. In one, the dream opened with the dreamer in her wheelchair but later she was able to be without it, and run freely. One who had acquired visual impairment had a nightmare where she couldn't see during a time of threat and panic, but her sight, including colour, returned before the dream ended.

It was especially surprising for me, knowing the usual boundaries on the body movement of each of those people, to hear about their dreaming activity. One woman, who in waking life is visually impaired and has painfully arthritic legs, was on a platform dancing a lively and energetic Scottish reel - not with the requisite seven other dancers, but with only one, a person she knows well who is also visually impaired. The man with a prosthetic leg in waking life was clambering around sloping turrets on the roof of a gothic castle. A woman paralysed as the result of a spinal injury was swimming and diving.

In the dream records I had collected over that six-week period from disabled dreamers, their dreaming selves, in almost every dream, functioned differently from their waking bodies.

The second set of results

I decided to follow these findings by engaging thirteen non-disabled counsellors in a similar dreaming project, in order to compare and contrast their experiences of the dreaming self with those of the first group. They gave me a total of 43 current dreams. So, were their embodied selves doing in their dreams anything they would not normally be able to do in waking life? Out of the 43 dreams, 37 gave a record of their bodies acting as they could in waking life. That meant that only in about 7% of those dreams were their dreaming selves felt to function differently from their waking bodies.

Some examples of where their bodies had different capabilities or physical limitations than they experienced in waking life: one experienced herself as a teenager in one dream. Another walked faster than a bus in one dream then in a second - a bit like Superman - caught an elderly patient falling from her hospital bed by diving onto the floor under her at precisely the right moment. Within one dream a woman caught and safely threw away a dangerous snake, and at tennis hit a ball high over a boundary fence to bounce on the roof of a red mini, then repeated the action precisely! The most spectacular difference from real life was in a dream where a woman's frail elderly father had submerged himself with his Land Rover in a deep pool but she, with his help, was able to haul it to safety by reaching down from the bank[4].

Taking stock

At this point in my research I felt I had the following facts to carry forward on this journey of discovery:

- It is usual for some disabled people to experience their dreaming self-image as having a non-disabled body.

- Sometimes non-disabled people also experience a dream self-image as having a body with capabilities

different from that of their waking life, but this does not seem to be a norm for most.

- The norm for all dreamers (in this first part of the study) was to dream of having bodies both able to move freely and with their senses functioning well.

Since before my formal study began I had been recording my own dreams, and at this time counted that in around 90% of dreams, my self-representation had a body doing what I could and usually might do in waking life. In the other 10%, my dreaming body was sometimes disabled, but sometimes super-abled! I had recorded 78 personal dreams by the time I gathered the dreams of the two groups of able and disabled people discussed above.

The study could have finished here, but instead had merely whetted my appetite to know more. I wanted to discover why this should be.

Over the next two years I asked ten additional disabled people, whose lives encompassed a greater variety of physical impairment than the original group, to discuss their current dreams with me. Their contribution added new dimensions to my work since they were people with a different life experience from those whose dreams I had already recorded: none were preparing to be counsellors. (NB: All 23 disabled dreamers who participated in my

[4] Some of those dreams are described in full later in this book

research studies were recognised in UK as disabled people.)

Here is an overview of the groups of dreams I studied, in the order in which I began to collect them from other people.

- 12 disabled counselling trainees along with one disabled staff member from LCIL who together contributed 35 dreams

- 13 non-disabled people in the counselling profession who contributed 39 dreams

- 10 additional disabled people, not counselling students, and living throughout the UK, who were willing to tell me current dreams for research purposes and contributed 33 dreams

- 9 of the original disabled counselling trainees were willing to contribute further dreams over a longer period of time and from them came 19 further dreams

- 6 further non-disabled people told me of dreams in which were people they knew in their waking life to be disabled people.

In addition, six other disabled people were willing to discuss the dreaming of disabled people from an informed stance; all gave me permission to incorporate information from interviews with them, into my work. Many people, when they knew of my interest, plied me with anecdotal evidence, all fitting the picture I was receiving from those who were formally engaged with me in my studies.

Pause for thought

Various chapters in this book deal with the discoveries made through studying the dreams I was given, the fascinating conversations I had with those who dreamed the dreams, and the conclusions at which we arrived about dreams and disability.

If you would like to explore this area for yourself as you read through the book, pause at each chapter's end and, if they might be meaningful for you, carry out the suggestions there for reflection and action.

Disabled people normally experience their dreaming self-representation as being non-disabled. In dreams they move and function freely.

Before you read what others have thought about this - why do you think this happens?

WHAT REASONS HAVE OTHERS GIVEN FOR THIS PHENOMENON?

The phenomenon of disabled people not having disabled bodies in their dreams is very well documented. Many researchers throughout the twentieth century have noticed this and tried to understand why it should be so. I expected to find the reason for this dreaming phenomenon by reading their work.

Wish-fulfilment

Just as the 20th century was about to begin, Sigmund Freud published his famous book *The Interpretation of Dreams*. One of his best known theories was that of wish-fulfilment: simply put, 'if you long for something it will appear, in some form or another, in your dreams'. Later in that century this became the most popular way for dream researchers to explain why disabled people usually appeared to have intact and fully functioning bodies in their dreams, and many people today still choose this explanation when they write on the subject.

Freud believed that dreams were very heavily disguised messages from the unconscious mind that had to be interpreted by a highly trained analyst. Would he have applied his wish-fulfilment theory to every incident of this particular phenomenon in the dreams of disabled people? I don't know, but I believe that this theory does not explain its occurrence in most dreams of disabled people.

Assumption behind this belief

The assumption that disabled people continually wish they were non-disabled people is largely unexamined.

I see myself as a non-disabled woman, and have a close friend who has had motor impairment from infancy. Often, over the forty years of our friendship, I have wished that she could move as freely and quickly as I could, and I have longed for and prayed that through some miracle her body would become as physically able as mine. I can understand why other non-disabled researchers have assumed that disabled people constantly wish they were non-disabled: after all, the way non-disabled people usually live their lives assumes that their bodies do whatever the majority of people in our country do! Their sense of worth and identity is often tied to their body image. It wasn't until I was working with several disabled adults that I realised that most were living contentedly in their bodies, getting on with their lives. When I began to study their dreams and explore with them what these might mean, I discovered that their dreams, as with non-disabled people, rarely focus on their bodies. We all dream about our relationships, our challenges, our current anxieties and fears, our life choices, our joys and losses, our transitions in life. At times when the condition of our body concerns us or gives us joy, then, and usually only then, that is when the body can become a focus of our dreaming.

Wish-fulfilment dreams in experiences of transition

People may suddenly become disabled as a result of an accident or illness. Others who have a degenerative physical condition sometimes find that it will quite quickly deteriorate after being in a very stable phase. In situations like these, naturally, the dominant wish of the individual concerned and of those who know and love them, is that the medical profession will be able to restore them to the level of mobility and sharpness of senses previously experienced.

Dreams during such a transition period can sometimes be understood in terms of Freud's wish-fulfilment theory, where in the dream the person sees and experiences him or herself back in their bodies as they used to function. With huge relief as they dream, they believe that their accident, illness or deterioration has been a nightmare from which they have now wakened. Such dreams are very similar to some experienced in any time of major transition, such as bereavement, separation and divorce, when it is usual to dream of life as it was before it changed.

Some would term these 'denial', rather than 'wish-fulfilment' dreams. Occasionally when people have been told for instance, that they will never walk again, they (very understandably) cushion themselves against the impact of such news, and go through a time when they simply deny the reality of what they have been told. In conversation with friends they will say things like 'I'll be back in the rugby scrum in three months', or even, 'I know the doctor said that, but I had a dream two nights ago where I was climbing Ben Lomond. I was completely healed. That dream was showing me my future.'

Such dreams pass. They are different from the dreams of those at home in their bodies who are managing the repercussions of impairment as one aspect of their lives. In their dreams their bodies are usually functioning well, but their bodies are not the focus of their dream.

Phantom phenomena

About half a century ago, Lawrence Kolb wrote in the *American Handbook of Psychiatry* a very comprehensive article on 'Disturbances of the Body Image.' Many researchers working in the psychological field refer to it. In it he summarised theories from various psychiatrists and psychoanalysts, and traced developments in thought about the concept of 'body image'.

Although various scholars differ slightly in what they include when they use the term 'body image', it is generally implied that each person carries around, in his or her mind, an image of how their own body looks, moves and functions, and the feelings they associate with having this particular body image in our society. Kolb (1959:750) wrote:

> The concept of disturbances in body image derives from observations of the affected individual's failure to perceive his body and its parts and adapt to them as they actually exist. The outstanding examples occur as a result of traumatic or surgical dismemberment, where the basic body image persists, despite the visible or apparent loss of a body part.

In the article Kolb addresses the issue of phantom phenomena, documented by a French surgeon as far back as the sixteenth century.

When a person loses an external part of their body in an operation or an accident, whether that be, for example, leg, finger, or breast, then they are likely to have a strange waking experience where they sense that body part is still attached to their body. They know it is not there, and they cannot see it, nor can they touch it. It's as if their mind is so used to having an intact body image that it continues to perceive it as whole and fully functioning. The term phantom phenomenon is also sometimes used to refer to experiences of movement sensed in a person where such movement is no longer physically possible - for instance, the movement of a limb or the erection of a penis.

Is this also a dreaming phenomenon?

These phantom phenomena are waking sensations, and so I was greatly surprised to discover that many researchers of the dreams of disabled people used this term to explain the dreaming phenomenon of having a body image that differs from a current waking body image. They sometimes call it a 'whole body phantom'.

This label may well be helpful to some people, but I find it confusing. People who experience waking phantom phenomena often do not find the experience pleasant. It can be associated with sensations of pins and needles, itching or even very severe pain in the area that no longer exists. Over the centuries doctors and surgeons, including brain surgeons, have tried various ways of ridding their patients of such odd sensations just because of the effects they can produce. But in dreams where the dream self is experienced as an intact and fully functioning body, such disturbing sensations are not felt.

Much is now known about the working of the brain, although much is still a mystery. One strange fact about waking phantom experience in people with whole arms amputated is that the phantom tends to alter significantly over time. Following an amputation a whole arm phantom may be experienced, but the phantom's size may eventually shrink till only a small phantom hand is felt attached to the existing shoulder! Neurologists tell us that in various parts of our brains there are maps of our body, each relating to and regulating specific parts of its functioning. Some body parts have larger areas on these brain body maps than others. Hands have larger areas on the brain body maps than arms do, but then hands do far more complex work with greater precision than arms. The phantoms for the areas that regulate less complex movements are the first to fade, but eventually the others usually vanish too. So when people with limb amputations are awake they know about the actual current condition of their body, and on occasions some of them have the additional experience of a phantom limb - either whole or partial. In their dreams, however, their norm as with other disabled people is that their dream body image is whole.

What is this body we experience in our dreams?

Paul Federn was known in the nineteen-fifties as an 'ego-psychologist'. The word 'ego' is the Latin word for 'I' or 'myself', and he specialised in exploring what it means for people to know themselves better: today we might say, to increase their self-awareness. For Federn, being able to say 'this is me' included knowing 'and this is not me'. He claimed that everyone had what he called a 'bodily ego' and a 'mental ego', and that these two ways of being aware of who you are, were different from each other.

Bodily ego

Before neurologists knew about brain body maps, Federn wrote that a person's 'bodily ego' was 'the continuous awareness of one's body'. He said that in our 'bodily ego' each one of us carries a picture of how we look, and of how our body is functioning. At any given moment we know if our senses are working well or poorly; we know if we have a headache or if a leg has gone numb, if we are feeling sick or well, hot or cold. We don't usually think much about it until we sense that something is not as it should be, but our 'bodily ego' is there for us when we need to think about our bodies.

Mental ego

His concept of the 'mental ego' was more a sense of the kind of person you believe you are: more to do with what we call personality - how we think, feel and react to what happens to and around us in life.

Federn claimed that although we are aware of both our bodily and our mental egos when awake, when we sleep we are aware only of our mental ego - of the kind of person we are - not of the condition of our physical body. In sleep, the only time we are aware or have a form of consciousness is when we dream. So Federn would say that when we experience our self in a dream, we meet only a symbol of our personality, not a symbol of the actual physical condition of our body.

I don't know why the dream researchers who were trying to figure out why disabled people had non-disabled bodies in their dreams paid no attention to Federn's theory. Perhaps it was because research on the human brain had not yet reached this point.

Most of the research I read was carried out and written up by non-disabled professional people. Where they ventured to give some interpretation to the dreams or to why the dreaming body image of a disabled person was different from their waking body image, these professional people seemed not to consult the actual dreamers. I discovered articles where researchers had no contact with the dreamers: they worked from collections of written records of dreams gathered by others, from people with the particular disability examined in their research project.

I had the privilege of working with each person who gave me their dreams, to help them discover what the dream might mean for them. I decided it was time I asked my original group of counselling trainees why they thought their dreaming body image was usually one of a whole and fully functioning body, and how they felt about it. I gave them a questionnaire and had a variety of answers. Here is a selection of their responses:

- 'I don't know'

- 'Well, it's the way I used to be'

- 'I've dreamt that way all my life: I'm used to it, so I don't feel it's odd'

- 'It gives me a lovely sense of freedom that lasts well into my day if it's been a good dream. When I was first disabled and dreamt that way I expected to be able to just jump out of bed. It was terrible to find that I couldn't. But I don't think or feel that way now'

- 'I think it's the way God meant me to be'

- 'It's just me'

- 'It's how I feel about myself'

These responses seemed to be quite a contrast to the main theories I had read about - with the exception of Federn's writing. Some of those disabled counsellors were describing very simply his concept of 'mental ego' with their words 'It's just me' or 'It's how I feel about myself'.

So, before venturing into the amazing field of neuro-psychology to read about the latest dreaming brain research, I decided, on the basis of my contact with disabled people, that Freud's theory of wish-fulfilment applied only to some of their dreams, in the same way as it did for non-disabled dreamers. I had serious reservations about phantom phenomena being the explanation for the absence of impairment in the dream body image of certain disabled people. There had to be another reason!

REFLECTION

If you are a disabled person, do you usually have a non-disabled body in your dreams?

If so, how do you feel when that happens?

3. RECENT NEUROLOGICAL RESEARCH INTO THE DREAMING BRAIN

This chapter outlines some of the thinking about the dreaming brain based on scientific research over the past half century, and seeks to explain why we dream as we do on the basis of the working together of only six areas of the brain to produce dreaming.

Be warned: because this chapter is fairly technical, some of my readers have said it requires more concentration on their part to follow it. It may, in parts, tell you more than you need or want to know! If this is your experience, skim through, read the summary, then move on to Chapter 4. There you'll find an explanation in a different style of most of what you need to know to work on your own dreams.

The dreaming brain

Most of the work I read was from people working, as I do, in the psychological field of human experience: people exploring how the waking human mind works. Unable to find a definitive answer to my question in the psychological approach to dreaming, I broadened my study to explore what is reckoned to be a more objective and scientific field of how the brain works, and how it influences what happens in the body.

Where was the answer?

Eventually I thought I had discovered a scientific explanation of the phenomenon I sought to understand. In 1953, two researchers[5] in their sleep laboratory discovered the existence of what became known as 'Rapid Eye Movement' (REM) sleep. The closed eyelids of their subjects during sleep would flicker for some minutes, and then resume normal stillness. Through a process of waking sleepers when this happened, they discovered this to be an indication that they were dreaming. So I read all I could find on REM sleep, and came upon this paragraph[6]:

[5] Aserinsky and Kleitman, 1953
[6] Melbourne and Hearne, 1999

An amazing characteristic of REM sleep is that the body's musculature becomes paralysed, although breathing is automatically maintained. There is active inhibition, so that only slight twitches are occasionally observed. Reflexes, such as the tendon reflex, are suppressed. The purpose of this paralysis would seem to be a protective ploy so that we do not physically act out our dreams!

Apparently[7] REM sleep begins with something happening in the brain stem at the top of the spinal cord. This cuts off the activity of the neurons whose task is to relay messages from the brain commanding muscles to move, so the body appears to be paralysed, although the genitalia in both sexes become engorged as we dream.

With the naivety of a novice I thought, this is it! If every dreamer's body is paralysed during dreaming sleep, and commands can't get through the brain stem to the muscles, then the sleeping brain of someone with an acquired disability might not be aware that their body now functions differently in any way from their body before it acquired impairment. But, if that were so: *why could people who had been born with motor impairment and had never been able to experience their body walking unaided, dream about such movement?* They would have no stored memories of their bodies moving freely.

There is a great deal to learn about the scientific study of the dreaming brain. Cycles of different levels of consciousness occur in our sleeping, and the cycles last for roughly 90 minutes each. The end of each cycle is marked by a period of REM dreaming. If, under laboratory conditions, a person's brain is connected to an electroencephalogram (commonly known as an EEG) to record the waves of electricity generated during sleep by brain cells, those four levels of consciousness show brain waves becoming slower and more relaxed. This suddenly changes as a period of REM sleep occurs. In REM sleep the brain becomes as alert as it is in waking[8].

Most sleepers have an average of five dreams during an eight-hour sleep, although they rarely recall the earlier dreams. Everyone knows from personal experience that most people do not easily remember their dreams unless they are particularly vivid.

Scientists still have not figured out why people dream! There are several theories about the purpose of dreaming, and in reading them I came to the conclusion that this might be because people use dreaming in many different ways. Certainly different cultures throughout the ages used the dreams of specific people to

[7] Dement 2001 and Fontana 1999
[8] Greenfield 1997

dream on behalf of the tribe or nation, to give warning or to seek guidance. Today in our culture, dreaming seems usually to be interpreted on a much more personal level. This is a humorous and insightful comment made way back in 1942 (sure to be received by many with great relief): one man[9] wrote that whatever the purpose of dreaming might be, it cannot depend on our remembering our dreams!

Current research on the dreaming brain

Someone referred me to the dreaming research carried out by Solms and first published in 1997 in his book *The Neuropsychology of Dreams*. Having borrowed this impressive academic tome from the British Library, I could not understand its highly technical language! I eventually sought the privilege of a lively and fascinating personal interview with Dr. Mark Solms.

Part of his research had been carried out by talking with patients in hospital who had damage in various areas of the brain. He talked with them about how they dreamed, and what had changed in the way they dreamed since the damage occurred. He already knew, from their medical and surgical records, which parts of their brain were affected. He

discovered a variety of experiences: some were now unable to dream; some now dreamed only in black and white; or that for some, nothing moved in their dreams. Dr Solms compared this new information with the discoveries of others, documented in historical medical records of each brain area affected. Eventually he established that only six areas of the brain are required to work together to produce the kind of dreaming most of us experience, and that if any of those areas were to become damaged in any way, the experience of dreaming would be affected.

Dr Solms listened while I told him of my attempts to try and discover why disabled people dreamed that their bodies were not disabled. When I hypothesised that it might be because of what happened at the brain stem to trigger dreaming and prevent muscles from receiving messages to move, he informed me that dreaming is not limited to REM sleep. Apparently dreaming occurs at other times during our sleep cycles - notably when we have just fallen over to sleep and when we are about to waken. These dreams (called non-REM dreams) are indistinguishable from REM dreams in the accounts dreamers give of them, yet when they occur the brain stem is not involved and so the muscles of the body are not prevented from moving during them. Bang went my theory!

[9] Lowy, 1942

This knowledgeable man was not about to spoon-feed me the answer to my question. He told me that he too had become aware of the phenomenon of non-disabled body-image in the dreaming of his disabled patients, then proceeded to hand me, as it were, some building blocks with which I might construct another hypothesis.

He told me there were body-maps in the brain to regulate various bodily functions, and that some of those operate even while we sleep, to maintain, for instance, the beating of our hearts circulating blood around our bodies, or the functioning of our lungs so that we continue to breathe. These work away in the background whether we are awake or asleep without us having consciously to will them to do so, thereby keeping us alive.

Using language from the computer world Dr Solms talked about areas of the brain that come 'on-line' during dreaming, while other parts that can be so lively and involved in our waking consciousness remain 'off-line'. Then he said that among the areas of the brain 'on-line' that network together to produce dreams while we sleep, there is no body-map available to enable us to be aware of the actual here-and-now physical condition of our bodies. (Yes - that's a sophisticated version of what Federn had thought fifty years ago: no awareness of our 'bodily ego' in sleeping!) Presumably, while

we sleep and dream, we don't need to know what's happening in our actual body: we can let it take care of itself. We can surrender control, and let it relax. However, if we are currently anxious about our health or our mobility, our dreaming brain[10] is free to deal with that in its own way.

(This made me more interested in exploring further reading in psycho-neurology[11]. If you'd like to do the same, see the further reading section at the end of this book).

The brain's dreaming network

There are six named areas within the brain's dreaming network (for readers who like to know technical names, they are listed in the footnotes to the next few paragraphs). Any specific dream we experience is the result of a process in which these areas work together to create dream scenarios and other symbols, and produce the thoughts and feelings we have while dreaming.

It's now possible for scientists to watch this process in a laboratory using a Positron Emission Tomography (PET) scan that produces a very lively picture of our dreaming brain. Before a dream happens, something needs to arouse us from the unconscious state in which we experience dreamless sleep, into

[10] An expression of Federn's 'mental ego' that operates both in waking or sleeping
[11] Kaplan-Solms and Solms, 2000 and Solms and Turnbull, 2002

dreaming consciousness. What actually arouses us may be anything from a major problem we are having in our waking lives, to something relatively trivial in the scheme of things, perhaps an emotion or niggling memory left over from watching a favourite film on TV that evening. The arousal is not the dream, but is the trigger that initiates the dream, and probably comes through one specific area[12] of our brain.

Our interest having been aroused, our motivation for exploring a particular aspect or theme from the trigger kicks in. Just as in waking life each action we make is motivated (perhaps not consciously) by some thought, feeling or experience, so it is in our dreams. Our dream begins to roll because we are motivated by a need or desire to do something about that trigger. We are asleep, so all we can do in response to the motivation to explore is to create a dream. The motivation for any particular dream is supplied from another brain area[13].

Then, in addition to those two, there are four more areas of the brain that work together just like a network or a team, to create the story of any dream that forms when we are asleep. One of these four[14] has stored memories and provides basic material from which to construct our dream. Often our dreams will contain varied selections of people, thoughts, happenings, and/ or emotions left over from our having lived through the previous day, but they can also provide archival material from any part of our past lived or fantasised experience that is in some way linked in our mind to the issue presented in any particular dream.

Most dreams, although not all, have a visual component. There is a specific region of the brain[15] involved in the process of linking meaning with what we see, so that area is included in the brain's network for visual dreaming.

It seems that from the earliest records of humankind dreaming, people have wanted to know what their dreams meant. Dreams tell stories, but it is common knowledge that these stories should rarely be understood at a surface level - they have another, symbolic meaning. So the work of another distinct area[16] of our brain is to take the thoughts and feelings we have stored in our minds - the ways in which we understand our lives by making connections - and transform these into symbolic forms in dreams. So the people, animals, plants, forms of transport, buildings that appear in our dreams are each symbols that represent something to us in our waking

[12] The temporal limbic region
[13] The deep ventromesial frontal region
[14] The frontal limbic region
[15] The ventromesial occipito-temporal region
[16] The left inferior parietal region

lives. This area of the brain also networks with one[17] that provides us with the ability to hold visuo-spatial aspects in our working memory for a time. That's what makes meaningful things happen in the dream whether the dreamer is a disabled person or a non-disabled one.

Perhaps in a dream you climb a hill but never reach the top, although you try. When you wake you need to ask yourself - is that a picture of what is happening to me in my life just now? Am I trying very hard to do something that requires a lot of effort, but never seem to reach my goal? Perhaps in another dream you are holding a new baby in your arms. You might ask yourself, what is this new baby I am holding so close to me? Have I recently begun a new project that I'm keeping 'close to my chest'? So in our dreams space is used symbolically: in other words, there is symbolic meaning in the spatial relationship people and things have with each other, in how they interact together, and what happens to them in our dreams.

Dreams have their own language, but it's one we know

All through our lives we are in the business of trying to understand what's going on around us, and why. When we make a connection, we store it for future reference in our waking lives, and eventually in our dreams.

It is sometimes said that we are born with a brain, but each of us makes up our mind. We each form a unique formation of connective tissue - neural pathways - within our brain, linking parts of the brain with other areas. Inside our brains are countless millions of actual physical links that would be visible to a brain surgeon during an operation, but that surgeon would not be able to see the mind inside the pathways. Often people use the words 'brain' and 'mind' as if they were identical, but they are not. It is our mind that holds the understanding running through the connections we have literally formed for ourselves inside our brain structure. As we grow, some of those connections wither away because they no longer make sense to us and so we don't use them. Others are reinforced, grow stronger and develop many more connections with other brain areas as we understand more and more - or think we do! Some connections will be shared in meaning with other people, but many will be purely personal.

It's easy to see this development - making connections - taking place in the minds of small children who ask questions. Some time ago I shared the fostering of two little boys. The older one was two years old when I came

[17] The right inferior parietal region

home having had my hair cut short. He reached up, so I lifted him up in my arms to say hello, and he gently touched my hair. He said 'It's gone'. I explained about having a haircut, but he was on a different wavelength. 'Is it dead?' he asked.

From a previous experience about which we knew nothing, he had made a connection in his mind of concepts he was trying to understand - perhaps about people disappearing from his life and then being told they were dead? Being taken from his birth family and given to foster parents had radically changed his life. He was exploring his new situation to find out if his old connections still held good. Perhaps that became part of his dreaming that night; I don't know.

Dreams speak the language of the way we have made meaning in our waking lives. Each one of us has spent our lives making our own meaningful connections.

Answers - but is this the whole story?

In today's language we could say that in dreams we are experiencing a kind of virtual reality. And the bodies in dreams - our own, or those of other people - are virtual reality bodies; symbols that we need to interpret before we can understand what they mean for us. Here was the answer I had been seeking.

All dream bodies, whether the dreamers are disabled people or not, are symbols, not photographic images. In other words, they are probably symbols of how we are feeling about 'being me in my world right now'.

Those symbols, like any other dream symbols, can be interpreted - but only by the dreamer. Only the dreamer knows what is going on inside his mind: all the connections and associations to any symbol or metaphor that might appear in his dream story. Only the dreamer can know how she felt about being herself in her life at the time of that dream.

Is this the complete answer? What about people who are born disabled?

One big question still remained unanswered. *If each person has his or her own internal dreammaker, fashioning dreams from their experience and the connections they have made in their minds, how is it possible that congenitally impaired people, who have never experienced (for example) what walking freely feels like when they are awake - can do this in their dreams?*

I thought I had discovered two possible answers to this question.

An image hard-wired from before birth?

Some scientists who are investigating phantom phenomena in waking bodies now wonder if we have a virtual reality body image in a body map hard-wired into our brains from before birth. This could explain why, if a person loses a part of his or her physical body, they might still retain a whole body image in their mind, which would include how the lost part of their body felt and moved. Although, as far as brain scientists know at present, there is no body map of the condition of our current body on the dreaming brain network, the virtual reality body image (if it exists) might just be available there. It could overlap with other brain networks such as the network producing phantom phenomena[18].

Mirror neuron activity?

This is the other hypothesis, presented with an anecdote. The explanation could lie in mirror neurons, discovered first in cats near the end of the twentieth century, and then in human beings.

One young woman who took part in my research had been born with motor impairment. Her leg muscles were not able to bear her weight. When she reached toddler stage her father constructed a sling on wheels so she could have the joy of pulling herself around on the living room furniture in a supported upright posture. Eventually she was able to manoeuvre her own first tiny wheelchair. She was a cherished only child and had never seen another disabled person until at the age of five she attended a school for disabled children.

There she was confronted by sudden awareness of her own impaired body by seeing other children in a similar condition. At five years of age she rejected this identity and decided that 'disabled' was for other people, not for her. Many children born disabled are brought up in families and communities where the sole formative image they see of the human body is of the non-disabled bodies of the majority. Why should they not identify with what they see and experience before they learn that others label them as different?

Everyone has mirror neurons in their brain. These neurons help when we are learning to perfect movement in dance, athletics, sport, even the smaller movements likely to be involved in craftwork. We watch the bodies of other people making certain movements, and without our consciously realising it, it has been discovered that our own muscles respond by mirroring the actions we see, even when we are apparently sitting still. When we watch other people move, mirror neurons fire in our brain, informing our muscles in such a way that we know how that movement would feel in our own bodies were we to replicate it. Have you ever watched someone fall, realised just how he or she would feel, and even said 'Ouch!'?

People born with motor impairment but who can watch others move, will, at some level, have the experience of knowing through these

[18] Ramachandran & Blakeslee, 1999

mirror neurons, how it feels to move, and therefore will have that memory available to them on the dreaming network in their brain. People who have watched birds fly, and followed the graceful movements in films of Peter Pan or Superman, know how to fly in their dreams!

No doubt in years to come, those working with the mind and the brain will discover many even more marvellous things about dreaming.

Summary

Research into the dreaming brain has located only six areas within the brain that work together to produce dreams. None of these has yet been shown to hold a realistic image of how our physical body looks and functions on that particular dreaming day. All dreams while we sleep are resourced from the networking of those same six brain areas.

When any person identifies someone in a dream as 'that's me', his dreaming self-image is likely to be a symbolic picture of how he feels about 'being me' in the dream scenario. The mind, inside the physical brain connections of each individual alive, has a set of unique connections and associations. These have been formed, added to and refined as we have grown, developed and learned from our personal experience of life. Interpretation of our dreams comes from the associations we have laid up in our minds over the years.

REFLECTION

You have read what others have discovered about the dreaming self-image - does it fit for you, and the way you dream?

4 MEET THE DREAM TEAM:
the six parts of the brain whose network creates dreaming

This chapter is especially for those who decided to accept my invitation not to become bogged down in brain research theory, but I hope all who persevered and read it right through will read this too. It gives a more imaginative approach to the neuro-scientific findings about the dreaming brain.

In the course of my research many people shared with me dreams of very difficult times in their lives. Perhaps some dreams were so vivid and easily recalled just because of the psychological pain in them. Some of my own most memorable dreams were from such periods in my life. They live on in my mind, but I also have a written record of them, of what was going on in my life when I dreamt them, and of how I interpreted their meaning. I want to use one of these to illustrate dream theory, so I'll use a real situation from a very personal part of my past, with a real dream, and weave it into a story.

How do dreams come about?

When we go to sleep, most of our brain takes time off work, perhaps to have a rest. A few parts remain on duty to keep us alive and in good working order, and every so often a small team of six rather creative parts gets together to provide us with the entertainment we know as 'dreaming'. I'll call them the Dream Team, and name mine as Jamie, Joanna, John, Jocelyn, Josie and Jan.

Meet my personal dream-producer, Jamie. He has to work in rather a stylised fashion, because he doesn't have access to the parts of my mind that think most rationally, but he considers that a challenge rather than a limitation. Jamie always seems to be entirely familiar with what has been going on inside my mind. He has to be, because he is responsible for producing these dream creations solely for me. From him comes the decision to produce each and he motivates the rest of the team. No one else has the privilege of viewing my dreams, so his productions are specially geared to this audience of one, and therefore to my needs. He decides on the theme, communicates this to the creative staff members that live with him in my sleeping mind and they work together on the plot while I sleep. Jamie chooses topics he believes to be just right for me at that moment. I've learned to trust his judgement about my needs.

Mind you, Jamie's very close to Joanne who constantly and with wonderful empathy tunes in to my emotional state, and keeps him in touch with this. One of Joanne's tasks is to suggest how best to represent me to myself in my dreams! She's got to come up with the image of a character with whom I can identify. Whether that character is female or male, young or old, living in the past or the present, and in whichever clothes she dresses me, I have to be able to sense immediately 'that's me'. And I do know that's me because whether I'm watching the body language of my dream image, or living within the skin of a particular image in the dream, this shows me how I am feeling about myself in the topic or theme of the dream.

John's my archivist, the keeper of my memories and all the associations I have attached to them throughout my life. He comes up with story lines and decides whether various dream scenarios for a specific dream should be from my childhood or from where I was yesterday, whether they should be from a book I once read or a film I've seen, or even from my fantasy life. Actually, he's not too keen on just repeating an old memory. It feels much better to him if he has a 'pick and mix' selection. He works very closely with Jocelyn, who is in charge of the props.

Jocelyn hoards. As soon as she knows that a person or an object has any meaning for me, she collects appropriate images and files them away in her computer along with associated sounds, colours, touch, smell, taste and so on. She's so competent on her computer that she can play with any of those images to convey precisely the impression she wants when she uses them. Jocelyn thinks symbolically, and teams up with John to give immediate access to whatever person, thing or scene will serve to remind me of what the team wants me to know, when I later reflect on my dream.

John and Jocelyn know that I am a visually oriented person: what I see makes a greater impact on me than what I hear, so they make certain that Josie and Jan are included in their team discussions. Josie is an expert in the visual aspect of life, and knows precisely what shape, colour, texture, or movement is most likely to catch my dreaming eye, but John and Jocelyn won't permit her to use anything unless it also has an association for me. Jan works with her, organising the moves in the drama (like a choreographer) - who does what with whom, how the characters and other props interact with each other - while Jocelyn checks to make certain that all I see, hear, touch, smell and taste produces the necessary emotion and still feels significant to me once I am awake. Dreams are produced by teamwork.

Lights, music, action - constructing a dream

It doesn't surprise me in the least that Jamie was motivated to send me a dream that night three years ago. I was distraught beyond comforting because my sister was dying and she no longer had the energy to talk much with me. To my mind it shouldn't have been like that: she was six years older than me and was to be there for me always, as she always had been. There was so much I still needed to talk through with her - but now I couldn't. When I wasn't with her, I was trying to cope by putting on a brave face, continuing with my work, and by telling as few people as I could what was happening in my life in case I lost emotional control.

Joanne sensed that I couldn't go on like this much longer and Jamie decided he had to call the team together to create a dream that might help me face up to the consequences of how I was handling this situation.

So John the archivist speedily reviewed thoughts and memories of past experiences in my life, my fantasies, all those connections my mind had made over the decades to make sense of life as I lived it, wondering which to select. Joanne was at his elbow reminding him of my understanding of the person I believed myself to be, and how I was feeling at that point. Along with the others they selected a list of characters, some of Jocelyn's props, a location or two; they had to get the emotional content right - and perhaps to create sound, dialogue, and, of course, Jan wanted metaphor in symbolic movement. Josie was concerned lest I might view what they produced and promptly forget it - she didn't want that to happen. This one had to grab my attention.

They couldn't just do a straight re-run of what had happened to me that day. (A set of guidelines exists that allows that only in specific circumstances.) They had access only to the resources stored within a limited section of my brain: so there were 'no go' areas. They were allowed to let me experience through any of my dream senses and could put me vividly in touch with my emotions, but only by using symbols and metaphors in this stylised production. And these had to be selected carefully for their power to suggest: they shouldn't show too obviously what was worrying me. They had to find symbols I could interpret, story lines that would indicate what was happening inside me. Listen in to my imagined dialogue of their team discussion:

Jamie: Let's think, now… Jean's going blindly ahead, believing she's in control, but she's not… how can we show her that?

John: How about putting her in her car, driving dangerously down a winding lane with high hedges on either side?

Joanne: No, that's not quite right, because that's not how she's feeling - it's more as if she's cruising numbly on automatic pilot. She's feeling lost, she doesn't know where she's going…

John: Well then - what about putting her on a coach with someone else driving?

Jan: Yes, that's more like it… and she won't know where the coach is going, but she'll just let it take her, she'll hardly care where.

Jamie: Good, that's Scene One - that fits. Do you agree, Joanne? Is that a metaphor of how her life feels to her at the moment?

Joanne: Yes, I do agree. What should happen next, then? Perhaps the coach could stop? Jean needs to stop coasting along, trying not to show her feelings.

John: What would she be likely to do when she gets off that bus?

Jan: She would want to know where she was. She's not a person who values being lost… she'll want to get back in control and make herself feel better.

Joanne: But we can't let that happen in her dream, because those desperate feelings are not going to go away for some time. Maybe we could introduce a few symbolic characters - ones that look as if they might promise help and comfort, but don't?

Josie: We could use a passer-by, a stranger. She could ask him where she is.

Jamie: But where might she want to be?

John: I know - with her friend in North Berwick, this friend is such a safe, motherly person for Jean.

Joanne: But we can't let her get there because she's got to face up to the fact that she's not receiving the comfort she needs.

Jocelyn: Life feels very strange to her at the moment. What about another stranger that might symbolise something for her - a young mother with a small daughter?

Joanne: Yes - she could see in that little girl that she's feeling just like a child, needing a mother.

Josie: And it could be lunchtime; she's starving for comfort. Will we let her have a banana - a good comfort food for a child?

Jocelyn: Well, maybe… But we need another prop - something that will really grab her attention and bring home to her that she needs to let go and be looked after by those close to her. She can't go on denying this need, shutting others out: she needs support.

Josie: Hey - what about a wheelchair?

Jan: Yes, that's it! These days, wheelchairs feature so much in her working life. Should we sit her in a wheelchair?

Joanne: Well, no, sitting in a wheelchair would not be the correct metaphor - she's not there yet… she needs support, but she isn't taking it yet.

Jamie: Right - the way we use the wheelchair in the dream ought to symbolise that. That's it. Her dream's ready to send. Here goes!

JEAN'S DREAM

Well, I did remember the dream the team sent me. It's still vividly there in my mind's eye. When I woke I wrote it down. Here is the dream as I dreamed it:

I was travelling somewhere on a coach with other passengers. It was lunchtime, and nothing was arranged for lunch. I was carrying a folded wheelchair with me and wondered what I should do. I decided to ask how far it was to North Berwick, because I would be welcome there. A kind-looking man said it was five miles away. I felt I couldn't manage that distance, propelling myself in the wheelchair, even if the road was flat. I joined a mother with her little daughter and we went to look for a snack followed by a banana.

The interpretation

After recording the story I had attempted an interpretation. Here's what I wrote:
I feel sorely disabled emotionally, too exhausted to reach someone who might comfort and look after me. I'm part of a coach party of strangers; no longer in control behind the driving wheel. I can't comfort myself - I need to borrow someone else's mother. I need an emotional wheelchair - but the one I am carrying is one I would have to summon up enough energy to move forward under my own steam. I have no steam left.

Jamie had used the dream team's collaborative creativity to hit the mark. I could acknowledge my feelings. I knew I needed support. I had to allow others to support me by sharing with them what was happening in my life. I could stop believing that I was able to carry on life as if nothing was happening.

REFLECTION

If you have already begun to try to interpret your own dreams, and are recording them, you'll probably find it useful to explore the various aspects of the dream with the scientific research in mind[19].

Here's a list of aspects to consider:

- The dream's context (what is happening in your life and passing through your mind)

- The motivation for having the dream (likely to be close to the theme of the dream)

- The emotions in your dream

- Your particular body image in this dream

- Other symbols in the dream and their associations for you

- Any metaphors in the interaction you sensed between the symbols

If you are not used to thinking what your dreams might mean, let me introduce this to you stage by stage.

Understanding dreams

Some of you will not have given much serious thought to how you might go about interpreting your dreams. As you read on through this book, I'll suggest various questions you might ask yourself to build up competence in understanding many of your own dreams.

You might also try using your growing understanding to help others understand theirs better by asking them the questions - but don't attempt to do this before you practise on your own dreams, and since you don't live in their minds, don't do their interpretation for them!

Many of the examples I will give will be from the dreams of disabled people, but the same guidelines and suggestions will be useful to all in interpreting either your own dreams, or to help others look at theirs.

---

[19] You might find it helpful to follow the structure given in Appendix 1

5. LOOKING FOR MEANING IN DREAMS

Does dream content differ for disabled people and non-disabled people?

When I completed my first two dream collections - the dreams from disabled trainee counsellors, followed by those from counsellors and trainees who are non-disabled people - the first question I asked myself was 'Is there any essential difference between the two collections? Would anyone reading through them realise that some dreamers were disabled people and others non-disabled people?'

Instead of noticing differences, I began to spot similarities between the two collections. For instance, right away I could pair together four dreams from each group as having some very similar symbolic images.

Comparisons of dreams

I paired the dreams of two women, one a disabled person and the other not. Both in the past had been nurses and eventually became ward sisters. In their dreams both were back in that sphere of work, but no longer in charge, and both had difficulty respecting the nurse who was in charge. Rather alarming yet different things happened in those wards for both dreamers.

One non-disabled and one disabled man both dreamed they were in an industrial site that was still under construction. The non-disabled man is a self-employed person and was being driven by car through the site in his dream. The disabled man, who had left work because it had become impossible for him to continue, was searching the site on foot in his dream, but eventually looking back down at it from higher ground.

In the dreams of another two women, both had a dream symbol in bright shining green. For the disabled woman this was a little artificial Christmas tree she pulled from a cupboard, while for the other it was a pair of bright shining green walking shoes that someone had left behind in a tramcar.

And finally, here are the two dreams I thought were most alike in their symbolism. I will report these as they were given to me, and also share some background about what was happening at that time in the life of each dreamer.

RUTH'S DREAM

What was happening in Ruth's life at the time of her dream?

Ruth has a degenerative condition. The muscles of her whole body, her limbs, her internal organs, and even her speech muscles, were progressively losing tone. She was facing a new phase of living, in fact, a major life transition.

For years her power chair had enabled her to go where she chose and at her own pace, but around that time it was becoming a more dangerous mode of transport for her. As she grew unable to manage the fine muscle control to regulate its speed and direction, she realised she would eventually have to abandon it. Along with it would go the part of independent living it represented. She had already thought ahead, and knew that her next chair would have to be controlled by others, and transported in a car driven by others.

This is the dream - as Ruth sent it to me by e-mail:

It was a beautiful dry, sunny day.
I was on my own in my power chair, beside a loch, on a high bank. Flowers, slight breeze, birdsong. Looked over the edge -
saw deep water ahead,
lovely sandy beach to right. But realised I had gone too near the edge. The chair toppled into the deep, clear water, but I STAYED ON THE BANK!
(This didn't seem at all strange in the dream!)
I looked into the deep clear water -
the chair was lying folded on a rock - it looked OK(!).

I thought of Dad paying for my car.

It was a kind of country park like those I knew with paths at **different levels** and I ran along shouting, 'I need some help'. A young girl with short fair hair shouted, 'I'll help'. I wondered how she'd manage, but was conscious of **feeling weak** and **tired**, and that we would have to try between us to get it out.

We ran back - she said she wasn't feeling well - time of month.
When we got to the spot, I realised she had no idea how heavy it was, and thought we could just lift it out. I told her we would need ropes...

then I woke up!

We worked face to face on the dream interpretation. Ruth understood her dream symbolism, but its meaning was not obvious to me until she described her forthcoming transition. There were significant metaphors in her dream: 'I saw deep water ahead' and 'I realised I had gone too near the edge'. That chair was a powerful symbol of what was happening in her life: it was in deep water and lying folded on a rock. She longed to return to what the power chair symbolised for her (she wanted help to raise the chair from the deep water using ropes), but knew that was impossible (the dream ended with the chair left on the rock in the deep water).

'Who is the other woman in the dream for you?' I asked. Ruth recognised that the other woman resembled a person she knew, and described her to me as one who does not take much care of her personal appearance. Ruth is the opposite, always well groomed and attractively dressed - but with her progressive loss of muscle control, that dream image symbolised her concern that she might become like the woman in her dream. No one else but the dreamer could possibly have known the significance of the symbolic presence of that other woman in the dream.

I was struck by the dream setting being so calm, beautiful and apparently familiar to her, but I knew Ruth had faced up to progressive stages of physical deterioration time and again and had helped others do likewise. The dream's emotional context, though another painful phase in her life, was familiar. Despite facing deep water, there was peace around her from accrued hard-won experience and a genuine spirituality. The power chair, a symbol of her independence, had been left on a rock, which for her was a symbol of God's dependability.

RUTH'S DREAM

CHRISTINA'S DREAM

What was happening in Christina's life at the time of her dream?

Christina is a non-disabled woman. She was aware that, at the other side of the world, her father was dying. He was very ill, and she planned to travel to be with him soon. As the eldest child, she knew his role as the head of the family would pass to her. She and he had always been emotionally close, and she dreaded facing the deep-water experience of losing him. Her recent visits had managed to pull him temporarily out of the depression linked to his illness.

Christina described to me her dream scenario context: 'The dream with Dad was quite obscure in lots of ways and I only remember one section of it. When I'm there with him I often go out on the farm as a spare pair of hands in a very ropey old Land Rover, and there's a stretch of shingle road that runs from the house, parallel to the coast down toward the neighbour.'

Here is Christina's dream told in her own words:

In my dream there was a patch of pine trees - a sort of plantation - down on our right, and we did some pieces of **work on a paddock** down one side of the pine trees, and then we came back towards the house, and stopped. And there was a big pond of water

(which doesn't exist actually. It was there in the dream)...

So we came back to this water on the shingle road and Dad said he was going to get out and walk across a boggy piece of land to fix something over there. He would take his tools with him and I would take the Land Rover and go through the gate and round the edge of the pond and across a bit which he said I would be able to ford in the Land Rover.

And I was looking at that, thinking, 'I really don't want to do this. I think the water is too deep and I'm scared of doing that by myself.'

But anyway, he was **adamant** that that was what he was going to do, and what I **needed** to do.

And then I slipped from that piece of dream where I was worrying about how I was going to manage with this and if I was going **to say 'no' to Dad** and whether he should be walking across that piece of land because he's pretty lame anyway, and suddenly the piece of water had a

steep edge

and the Land Rover had **slipped down** it, and Dad was in the water - under the water - and trying to push the Land Rover up. And I was on the edge seeking for a ledge to grab the Land Rover with, and to pull it. And between the two of us **we**

pulled the Land Rover out

(which would have been totally impossible).

And then we went back to the house which was quite nearby, and my concern was whether he would have a **bath** to warm up, having been in the cold water, before he changed his clothes. And then I woke up.

···

As a researcher, I linked Ruth's symbol of the power chair with Christina's dream symbol of her father's Land Rover. Both seemed to represent continuing mobility for their owners, control and a meaningful independence. For Christina, the Land Rover was associated with her father. Experiencing both going into deep water was probably symbolic of what was happening to her father and his independence during his illness. His invitation to drive the Land Rover also symbolised for her status of the head of the family that he was beginning to hand over to her.

For both Ruth and Christina, the time 'on the edge' was a time alone. Christina's deep-water symbol was a pool not there before in her experience, in contrast to Ruth's. She felt fearful, knowing she would have to negotiate it alone when the time came, fearing that it was 'too deep' for her to ford by herself, and wanting to avoid it. That time did not arrive in this dream. She helped her father and the 'ropey old Land Rover' out of their deep-water experience, back to the safety and normality of home and a warm bath. That part of the dream seemed to reflect her past experience of helping her father come out of his depression.

Where do dream symbols come from?

The symbols that people had, in the dreams they shared with me, seemed to be a combination of the objects and people meaningful to them in their everyday living, or their memories of when these had been around in their lives.

Symbols and metaphors from the cultural background of the dreamer.

Although Christina had been born and brought up in New Zealand in a family of British origin, and Ruth was raised in Scotland, both these cultures share the descriptive metaphors of being 'on the edge' and of 'going through deep water'.

Ruth would have been unlikely to dream of 'working on a paddock' or being in a 'ropey old Land Rover' as Christina did, since these were not part of her everyday past or present experience, although of course, Ruth has heard of paddocks and has seen old Land Rovers in Scotland. Instead she experienced herself as being beside a loch in a country park and in her wheelchair.

I'm quite certain that in her youth, Ruth would have experienced 'walking over a piece of boggy ground', but that metaphor was to describe, in the dream of the farmer's daughter, Christina, the psychological experience of her father's long illness.

Part of the over-all cultural background of many people is their particular religious or faith experience. Symbols from these often appear in dreams of people going through painful transitional experiences where they are aware of the fragility of life and feel their need for help and support from beyond themselves. So Ruth's dream had the symbol for her of the rock from the Judaeo-Christian tradition.

Interpretation of symbols in dream

The more I worked with the dreams I was given, the more I appreciated that symbols could be interpreted only in context, and that the context was usually what was going on in the dreamers' lives around that time, and how they thought and felt about all of that.

I decided that it was no help to go through dream records searching for symbols exclusively used by disabled people and others for non-disabled people: dream symbols were drawn from the whole of life's experience, and not only from one aspect of it. (As you will see in the next chapters, I did become especially interested in the symbols that occurred in the dreams of both disabled and non-disabled dreamers where there seemed to be a direct link to some aspect of disability.)

Many people buy books that claim to give an interpretation of the symbols in their dreams. In one reputable Edinburgh bookshop I found nine books with a dream symbols' dictionary section. They all listed 'wheel', and a few had 'wheelbarrow' but only one had 'wheelchair' and it offered this:

> On the one hand, restriction, suffering and the inability to escape from problems. On the other hand, in spite of a psychological handicap, moving forward. Often such dreams are a challenge, in a sense, to learn to walk again[20].

At least this writer gave two possible and contrasting interpretations of this symbol and did not work on the basis of 'one interpretation fits all'.

In one of my own dreams around that time there were three naked and lively two-year old male toddlers. I was bending over them when one, with his back towards me, swiftly pushed his buttocks up nearly into my face. The skin on his bottom was covered in big red spots. In the dream I recognised him as a disabled man I knew quite well, although the dream toddler's body was not impaired.

Already confident I could interpret what his red spots meant to me, I flipped through the pages of another of the dictionaries for its interpretation of 'spots'. I was amazed, amused and puzzled to find myself reading that its authors thought it meant that I had money coming to me! I had no link in my mind between spots and money. I had described them in my dream record as 'angry red spots', and the little cameo with the aggressive thrust of body language right in my face gave me the same message! In waking life this man was angry with me, and I believe I dreamed of this so that I would 'face' up to that and do something about it… and I'm still waiting for the money!

The same symbols will often occur for a dreamer in several of her dreams. Because of this, some people make a list of their own dream symbol interpretations[21] rather than seeking their meaning in a dictionary. A list of dream symbols compiled by an external agent cannot possibly document the variety and nuances of meaning and associations you have in your mind, forged from your own experience.

I hope to show you that the work and sometimes fun of looking at what your own dream symbols mean to you is far more subtle and personal than can be supplied by a dictionary based on the dreaming experience of other people.

---

[20] Vollmar, 1997

[21] Guidance on making your own dream symbol dictionary is in Appendix 2

Summary

Dream symbols for all dreamers come from their experience of every aspect of their lives, including their cultural background. Only the dreamer knows for certain how to interpret her own dream symbols, because she knows the links that exist in her mind with those symbols.

REFLECTION

Recording and / or sharing dreams with a friend

You've seen how the dreams of both Ruth and Christina sprang from what was happening at that time in their lives.

You might like to record the next interesting dream you have, and see if there is a connection between it and what is happening in your life at the time.

Are you a person who would enjoy telling a friend about your dreams, and listening to theirs? Doing this with someone you trust and who knows you well can be good fun, and helpful. It generally works best if you are:

- interested in dreams

- willing to ask questions and try to answer each other's questions

- prepared to accept your friend saying 'I don't know.' 'I don't think so.' 'Let's stop there', or perhaps 'that was good. Your questions helped me. Thank you.'

If you'd rather go it alone then set off on the journey with this book in your hand.

6 THEMES IN DREAMS

It often helps in dream interpretation to look for the theme in any dream. It's too easy to get side-tracked - drawn into the parts of the dream that are fascinating and quite different from the dreamer's usual experience - and so, to miss the point.

A dream to learn from

Before you read this, I suggest you have a good look at the painting of Vevey's dream on the page 47. (The painting by John Lowrie Morrison was created from the dream description below).

VEVEY'S DREAM

From Vevey's dream record and its illustration, it would be impossible to guess that her body became paralysed some years ago. As the result of an accident she has no movement in her limbs and torso apart from being able to use one hand sufficiently well to control the joystick on the arm of her electric wheelchair. In order to live independently by herself in her own accommodation, she employs a total of thirteen part-time support workers or personal assistants around the clock on a weekly roster to do what she needs to have done by others. In this dream, the interaction between Vevey's self-image and the other images was a picture of a part of her waking life that worried her.

This is the dream as she told it to me:

I was standing at the edge of a swimming pool.
There were quite a lot of people around the swimming pool. I tried to attract the **attention** of my support workers, and for some reason they **couldn't seem to hear** what I was trying to say to them. They were walking further and further away. In order to try to attract their attention, and rather than trying to run round behind them
- I was able-bodied in the dream -
I decided I would **dive** into the pool, and swim to catch up with them. I did rather a good dive. I managed to clear the **entire length** of the pool in one dive! I swam right from one end to the other, the length of the pool.
And then I just repeated that, **diving into the pool** over and over again. Each time I did, I never managed actually to attract their attention. Everybody else was looking at me and cheering because I had **done so well**, and I was very aware of the pleasure of swimming through the water.

Vevey's dream was one of the first dreams I listened to from the group of disabled counsellors-in-training. It was a dream she enjoyed, and one I grew more and more excited to hear and discuss. I loved the picture of her wonderful dives and the crowds cheering her on, and that was what I responded to initially when she told me about it. I was totally fascinated by the contrast between Vevey's active dreaming self-image and the still body image I saw of her day by day in her wheelchair. I was so caught up with that, that I forgot to pay attention to the other symbols in her dream!

If you had a similar first response, I suggest that you read it again - as I had to - to discover why Vevey had this dream. Not until I was transcribing our conversation about it did I realise I had missed the motivation she had for

VEVEY'S DREAM

dreaming. In fact, her dream record showed quite clearly why she needed to dream it. I had overlooked her support workers ignoring her and walking away without being aware of her need to talk with them.

Support workers are a very big part of Vevey's life. These were as much a symbol of her current lifestyle as her wheelchair would have been, had it been in her dream. In this dream many people were cheering her on, communicating to her how wonderfully she was doing, but try as she might, she couldn't manage to have her support workers hear what she wanted to say to them. They were talking with each other, but walking away from her.

Those particular support workers were disabling her by not listening to her, keeping her dependent instead of increasing her ability to be independent. I knew from her telling me previously, that before her accident Vevey thought of herself as outspoken: she was young and lively; someone who regularly argued with those closest to her, and who freely expressed her own opinion. Her dream suggested something very different about her present style of communication.

What was Vevey's dream team trying to explore with her? The theme was clearly the lack of effective communication between Vevey and her support workers: her spectacular dives were a way of attracting their attention - but the support workers were not standing in the cheering crowd.

I contacted Vevey again to say I had noticed what a big part her support workers played in her dream, and asked her if what they were doing might be a metaphor of what was happening in her life just now. It was. She had grown afraid of giving them offence and losing their goodwill by telling them out straight 'Please don't do that. It would be better for me if you did this.' Understandably, it was easier for her to concentrate on the parts of her life she was managing very well, and to enjoy these.

Instead of helping her to interpret her dream the first time we spoke about it, it was as if I had identified with the crowd around the swimming pool, cheering her on - telling her how well she was doing and enjoying that with her instead of taking seriously the fact that the dream's theme was of a failed attempt to communicate. I had a lot to learn.

Vevey's internal dream-producer was saying to her, 'Vevey, you need to do something about this!' Vevey was training to be a counsellor of other disabled people, and her dream had highlighted an issue that is quite common for people who fear the possible repercussions of losing the goodwill of others for the smooth running of their lives.

REFLECTION

If you have begun to record your own dreams[22], you might find it helpful to:

- Record the date of the dream

- Record the story of the dream as you remember it happening, in as much detail as you can

- Stand back from it for a while, and consider what actually happened in the dream

- As you did before, ask yourself if you can see any connection between what happened in this dream and what is happening in your life at the moment, and in your thoughts and feelings about it all

- Then consider what might be the theme of this dream. 'What's it all about?'

- Finally, give the dream a title that catches the essence of the dream's message

Practice in finding titles

If this is something new for you, why not practise by finding a suitable title for Vevey's dream - one that summarises what it is all about? You may find that you need to step back a bit from the detail of the dream before you can see this clearly. When you've had a go, try looking at the suggestions below - but your title will be just as good as these if not better. Do try it out first by yourself!

If I were asking myself for a title for a dream, I would wonder - is there a thread of meaning running right through it - or what is the theme of this dream?'

When I decided that I could see one, I might try for a formal title like '*Trying to attract attention*' or '*The challenge to communicate*'.

On the other hand I might prefer a more informal style, perhaps something like '*I need you to see ME*', or ' *Why don't they listen to me?*'

The title you have chosen might use very different words, but could suit you better. Mine are only possible samples of how it might be done. Try it in your own style.

(NB: If storing your dreams on a computer, you could use the dream titles as filenames).

---

22 This is set out as a structure in Appendix 1

7. ARE WHEELCHAIR USERS IN WHEELCHAIRS IN THEIR DREAMS?

Perhaps another question first: 'Are car drivers in cars in their dreams?'

When I compared the dreams of non-disabled people with those of disabled people, more cars featured in the first group than did wheelchairs in the other. Although some of the disabled dreamers were also car drivers, non-disabled drivers were in all the dream cars in that sample, and it was interesting to hear what happened in their dreams. Their cars were involved in accidents, paintwork was scraped up both sides of one whilst in a car park, another was overturned, one wouldn't start, some encountered road blocks… It became increasingly obvious that what happened to a car in the dream was often a metaphor of what seemed to be happening psychologically to the dreamers in their waking lives, especially in their relationships. In dreams, the car - not the dreamer's body image - sustained the damage!

The wheelchair as a dream symbol

Ten wheelchair users shared their dream records with me. They all without exception had dreams where there was no sign of a wheelchair, but on occasion, in the dreams of a few, a wheelchair was very much in evidence.

Ruth's dream (see p.37) featured her wheelchair, although she was in it only at the beginning of her dream. The wheelchair was not there principally to transport Ruth but to symbolise something that was happening in her life.

DANIEL'S DREAM

Daniel is a disabled man very much involved in his local church and community. He was willing to tell me his dreams, but sometimes resisted attempts on my part to discover what he thought they meant. Born with cerebral palsy, he had been very active and had excelled in sports for disabled people, but following an operation some five years before I met him, had become a power-chair user. He felt that his speech was not distinct enough to communicate with me directly, so asked his wife to be interpreter. On one memorable occasion, with Daniel sitting beside her, she read to me over the phone a dream he had dictated.

This is his dream, as dictated to me over the phone:

I was going up the street, when S's father (they come from India) invited me into her house.

He said to me, 'I've got to go out, so would you sleep with S?'
So I got into bed with her and she started poking me, and I thought, 'Is this some kind of cultural ritual?' I fell asleep, and then because I'd fallen asleep, when I woke up I began panicking because I thought I'd 'slept with her'.
I was still with her, not with my wife. I began to panic.

I couldn't see where I'd put my socks - one sock in particular was missing. When I found it, you'd think I'd found gold
I was so relieved to get out of the situation. And my wheelchair, I could feel as I was going down the road to home, started jumping for joy.

DANIEL'S DREAM

Interpreting the dream

I asked what he thought the dream meant. It was probably to be expected, in the situation of the dream being told, that I got the response: 'A load of rubbish!'

I shifted to safer ground and invited his wife to ask him if he could say any more about what happened to his wheelchair. He responded:'When I got into it, it seemed to go like Fred Astaire.' I asked how that felt, and he responded that he was glad when it stopped and he arrived home. I decided not to press for any further possible interpretation. After all, he was helping me with my research at this point rather than asking me to help him interpret his dream, but I suspect all three of us enjoyed the telling of the story!

Sometimes wheelchair dreams occur regularly for a while

JEZ'S DREAM

Jez has multiple sclerosis, and when eventually a wheelchair was recommended for her use she welcomed it. She had grown weary of her struggle to maintain mobility. Sometimes the mere thought of going through the process of getting herself to somewhere she would love to be was so challenging that she stayed at home. She remembered having a dream from about a year before my research began where she walked, skilfully pushing her wheelchair around various obstacles in their path. There was so much she wanted to do with this new lease of energy it provided, and together she and her wheelchair seemed a winning team!

What was happening in Jez's life at the time of her dream?

Jez is a vivid dreamer with excellent dream recall. She previously belonged to a Jungian dream group, and often records and analyses her dreams. When she contacted me with the dream she wanted to share, she had just been through a period of emotional upheaval where wheelchairs were greatly in evidence in all her dreams. She was considering a new plan for her future - a major undertaking - and explained this to be the background to her dream.

It was long complicated dream that took time to unpack. This was part of the dream as she told it to me:

I get frustrated or held up, and I decide to go back up to my room to get something or other and it's several flights up wide shallow stairs and there, at the top of a wide stair which is really a sort of landing

- there, abandoned - is my wheelchair.

I remember that on my way down I decided not to go down the stairs on it, because going downstairs would seem potentially dangerous. But I did think at that point

'I'm probably going to need it at some stage when I get tired.'

But I notice that its diagonally opposite wheels - it's the wheels I'm concerned with, they are the same size, and quite small, like old fashioned pram wheels - and two of them, diagonal ones, had come off.

Try as I might, I couldn't seem to snap them on again.

They're supposed to snap back on, but they won't, so I have to leave the chair, but I reckon I can get help to sort out the problem later.

I waken feeling I will have to sort this out at some stage.

Jez was keeping the wheelchair there in case she needed it. The pram wheels symbolised dependence on the wheelchair - as a baby would be dependent on her pram - and she realised that the ones that would not snap back on symbolised the repair needed by her support system.

I asked 'How do you think your dream challenges or informs you about that whole situation?'

Jez replied 'I'm not sure where the wheelchair comes in except for me to be aware that I'm not - I don't need to be totally under my own steam. I can do bits by myself, but I do need help and I'll make sure that that help is reliable and working…I think I need a wheelchair for some parts of me.'

Here the wheelchair is a positive symbol of something that gives Jez the help she needs to reach where she wants to go - but in the

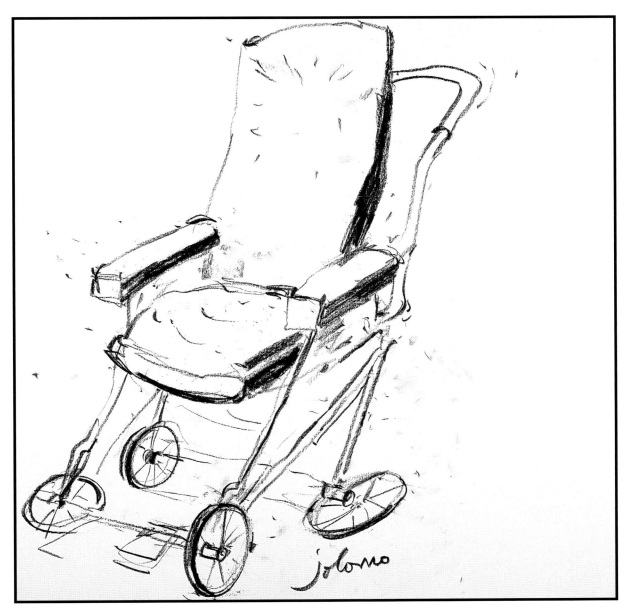

JEZ'S DREAM

dream, the wheelchair was disabled! When in her dreams Jez and the wheelchair are working happily together as a team - Jez walking behind it, influencing its direction - she is coping well. Nothing disables her. She has what she needs, to go where she wants. Her support system is in place, within her control. When in her dreams someone else controls the chair, or when the chair and she are separated, things also seem out of her control in her waking life: her physical disability becomes an issue for her, and sometimes a disabled wheelchair symbolises this. The more constricted her life feels, the more the wheelchair is disabled in her dreams.

Sometimes wheelchair dreams come occasionally

It was common in the dreams related by wheelchair users to hear that their dream wheelchair was empty, not in use, but present in the dream.

BETH'S DREAM

The effective functioning of the muscles of one of Beth's legs was affected by her having polio in infancy. Although she walked for years unaided, only in her dreams has she known what it is like to walk without some motor impairment. As the years have gone by her other body muscles and joints have worked hard to compensate for the leg that was shorter than the other. Beth also had several surgical operations, and her joints became increasingly arthritic.

She passed through a distressing emotional battle before accepting that she needed the help of a wheelchair. Struggling without one, Beth risked further wear and tear to her body. Even after the chair was delivered to her home, she could not bring herself to use it regularly. She believed it was a symbol for all to see that she had failed in her lifelong attempt to remain physically active and independent. Since starting to use her chair, Beth could not recall it appearing in her dreams.

In one recent dream Beth was celebrating with good friends, dancing freely with her husband, and thoroughly enjoying herself. They were at a seaside hotel for the weekend, and after dancing, walked hand-in-hand barefoot along the beach under the stars. It was wildly romantic for her. The dream location switched. They were back home walking together into their own bedroom, and facing them was a wheelchair! She awoke, shocked and insulted by that image, and phoned to speak about it.

'Why now?' she demanded, sounding querulous. She wanted her wheelchair to remain out of her dreams.

'What does a wheelchair symbolise for you?' I asked.

'That I have no control over my life - well, the physical side.'

'Could there be any significance for you, in the wheelchair being in your bedroom?' The whole tone of her voice altered as she was overwhelmed by suddenly realising its significance. She began to sob. 'Oh …the pain in my legs is so acute these days that we can't make love.'

Reflecting on the significance of wheelchairs in dreams

When Vevey began to tell me her dreams, there was no sign in them of her power chair (see p.45). Later came a few dreams where she was in her chair. She wondered if this might mean that she was more accepting of her disability, because she felt that her chair had become an extension of her body image in her waking life.

To her surprise, Vevey reverted to having more bodily active dreams without her chair. In one she was powerful, standing eye to eye with her sister, quarrelling on an equal footing.

Then, one day in her waking life, the joystick on her power chair came away in her hand. Her chair remained stable; she was not hurt. While it was away for repair Vevey had to revert to using a non-motorised chair with someone else pushing it. She didn't feel good about the way she presented herself under these conditions. She couldn't even use her adapted phone.

This triggered repetitive nightmares. In each, Vevey was in her power-chair reversing down a taxi's wheelchair ramp (as she did regularly in her life), when the joystick came away in her hand. The chair would topple backwards. Vevey's legs would fly wildly into the air while she shouted for help, but when the taxi-driver came to raise the chair and stabilise it, its normally solid structure would disintegrate beneath her. Vevey told me that this dream situation reflected what she felt about her life when she had to return to the helplessness of being in her old pushed wheelchair.

Vevey enjoys the process of thinking things through, so she wondered if falling backwards in those dreams had put her in touch with her body's memory of the original traumatic accident where she fell backwards from a height and wakened in hospital, paralysed, and with her life as she had known it till then, in pieces.

By the time I completed my research Vevey had still not reached a conclusion on the meaning for her of the dream wheelchair symbol. Does it appear when she feels helpless, out of control of her life - or could it be a sign that she has now accepted her dependence on it to the extent that it is an extension of her dream body image? Somehow it seemed a mixture of both. If Vevey settles for the latter, she will be an exception amongst the wheelchair users I have interviewed on this subject. As a researcher who is also a counsellor, I know it is essential not to impose what I might assume to be a general principle on any dreamer. The importance for any person who offers one of their dreams to another is to be valued, respected and if possible better understood, not for that other to come with a set of measures by which she labels and judges the dreamer's experience.

Summary

People who use wheelchairs in their waking life are likely to find them appearing occasionally in their dream life. Never assume that you know what a wheelchair means for another person. It would seem that a dream wheelchair symbolises different things to different people. When one does appear, something in the dreamer's waking life has often caused him or her to feel insecure, and that arouses strong - perhaps even emotionally disabling - feelings and thoughts.

If a wheelchair - or another form of transport you use, your car for example, appears in your dreams, it will be there as a dream symbol: it will have a significance that only you can truly interpret, and at different times in your life, its meaning for you might change.

REFLECTION

If you are a wheelchair user/ car driver:

- What does your wheelchair/car symbolise for you?

- Does it ever appear in your dreams?

If it does appear in your dreams, it may be there for a reason. When you have a dream where there is a wheelchair/car, ask yourself:

- What emotions did I feel in that dream?

- Am I feeling these emotions just now in my waking life?

- What was happening to the wheelchair/car in my dream?

- Could that be a metaphor of what is happening to me in my waking life just now?

Adapt this wheelchair image to your own life situation - a symbol other than a wheelchair might provide a similar reference point.

For instance, one woman who lived alone had similar dreams to those described above, but featuring her budgerigars. She was going through a particularly distressing time that had nothing whatsoever to do with her pets. She told me she depended on the relationship she had with them to give her joy and a sense of purpose in life: they were her support system.

8 DREAM SYMBOLS OF THOSE WHO HAVE ACQUIRED SENSORY IMPAIRMENT

Wheelchairs in dreams might represent a particular aspect of the lifestyle of wheelchair users, perhaps one engendering an emotional response. Would it be similar for those with other kinds of sensory impairment - would a guide dog engender the same kind of response for those with visual impairment? People who acquire sensory impairment have often been the subject of dream research. Is the change in their waking experience echoed in their dreams? The answer is not straightforward.

Visual impairment

Seeing or not seeing in dreams

Several people, born sighted, who have later acquired visual impairment, told me that it is common for people to ask them if they see in their dreams. It must be an area that fascinates many people, because I discovered that much research has been carried out and published about this, especially in North America.

I enjoyed listening to the dreams of the people who took part in my study who had acquired visual impairment, and I will offer examples from their dreams. But I also want to share some facts I learned through reading the research of others, and comment on the experience of two dreamers, which contrasted with that of the published research I had read.

Some research indicates that it is usual for people who have been visually impaired for some time to begin to dream less in visual terms, and to have dreams where their experience reflects only the senses they still use day by day. I did not interview any person who had acquired visual impairment under the age of five. Apparently it is uncommon for such people to retain into adulthood dreams with a strong visual component.

One report claims that it is rare for people who have been visually impaired for forty years to have a visual component in their dreaming, because by that time it will have faded till it is no longer present. It so happened that I had two women in my study who were both visually impaired more than forty years ago - one when she was eight, and the other while a young mother in her early twenties. Perhaps they are the exception to the rule, but the dreams they shared with me were still both visual and vivid. When I talked with them about that research finding, each was surprised to hear of what it claimed. It had not occurred to either that she might lose this capacity. Neither has been aware of any diminishing in the visual aspects of her dreaming, although not all their dreams are totally visual or even have visual components.

Both these women described to me independently how she had nurtured her ability to visualise during waking hours, perhaps thus keeping it alive. One shared how she loved 'seeing' her adult children's holiday photos. I asked her what she meant by that. 'Well', she said, 'when my daughter gets them back from the shop we sit down together and she describes each one to me in detail. I can visualise everything. I really enjoy it. It's almost as good as having been there myself.'

In one of her dreams, as she carried a baby up two flights of stairs, she dropped him. Appalled that she had let this happen, and fearing the worst, she ran swiftly down, and picked him up in her arms only to discover him unharmed. She knew the baby and named him. He was her son, now in his mid-forties. 'How did you know in the dream that it was your son?' I asked. 'Oh, he was born before I lost my sight, and he looked exactly in the dream as he did

then,' she replied. It was a dream produced by her anxiety for her grown son who was going through a difficult time, and where she was wondering if the strength of her mother-love for him would be enough to keep him safe.

The other woman, blinded[23] at eight years of age, recounted a current dream where she talked with a man new to their neighbourhood. 'And how did you know who he was in your dream? Did you recognise his voice?' I asked. 'Oh no! I haven't yet met this man. My husband has, and when he told me about him I asked him to describe him to me, and the man in my dream fitted that description,' she replied. Then she added, 'But of course, it's not only people you know that you see in your dreams.'

This woman regularly asks her family to describe to her what they see, and stores in her memory the visualised image she constructs in the process. Presumably, when any person has a visual dream, the visual part is based on memory of what they have seen, and on what they may have used their imagination to visualise.

Here is a verbatim extract from one of her recent dreams as she recounted it to me.

---

[23] I believe this term is no longer politically correct, but its substitute 'visually impaired' does not so accurately describe this woman's experience. I take the liberty in this chapter of using some previously accepted terminology.

I was sitting in the doctor's surgery and in front of me was standing a lady with **brown hair** shoulder length and straight, a green anorak and tartan skirt. The **odd** thing about it was that she was wearing tights and had a line going up the backs of her legs! And brown shoes.

In front of her, but facing me, so they were facing their mum, was a **boy and girl** - maybe about age eight or ten. The receptionist was over to my right. The lady had seen the doctor and had come back out and the receptionist said 'How are you?' And she said, 'This is a surprise, but we're very much looking forward to the baby.'

There was nothing to suggest this dreamer was not still a sighted person. A description like that left me in no doubt that what was being described to me was a dream with both vivid visual and auditory components recalled in detail. Visually impaired people live in a world of sighted people, and like them, regularly use sighted language. When I asked one why, he responded, 'Would you not think it rather odd if I were to say to you when we part, "*Hear* you tomorrow, Jean"?'

So I checked out with such dreamers their use of visual words in any dream description. Perhaps anticipating such a question, the dreamer quoted above added at the end of her description of the dream in the doctor's surgery, 'The lady's voice sounded as if she was maybe 40 or so. At no time did she face me.'

Are there any signs of impairment in the dreams of visually impaired people?

Would there be any sign in their dreams that they were no longer sighted people, I wondered? For instance, would their guide dogs appear in their dreams? Or would there be occasions in their dreams when they did not see? During the period of my study I was given nine dreams from women who had been born sighted, had later acquired visual impairment and who now have guide dogs. Only in one did a guide dog appear, and then it was out of harness, as a family pet and companion. It was interesting for me to note, however, that it appeared in a dream at a time of great emotional need in the family, when the dreamer's brother was terminally ill. In that dream she gave her mother the dog to take for a walk.

The guide dog - just like the wheelchair for some wheelchair users - was a symbol for her of dependable support when that was needed. The dreamer gave the dog to her mother because she felt her mother needed even more emotional support than she did herself. Guide dogs fulfil different functions in the waking lives of their owners. They are working dogs in harness for the world beyond the doorstep, but are in a more social relationship off duty or at home, when they can be so many different things to owners and their families, including a source of love and comfort.

The woman who acquired total visual impairment in her early twenties went through a time of looking back through her life, trying to understand why things had worked out as they had, and why people related to her as they did. She began to have a series of vivid dreams where she seemed to be clearing out the family home. In them she would fill rubbish buckets full, but bits and pieces of it would fall out again.

She had memories from her sighted childhood, of trying to understand what might lie behind a family secret. She could recall angry blaming words between her parents, and the feeling that she did not belong. Often ill as a child, she had felt abandoned in hospital. Whatever the family secret was, she feared it was her fault and explained this 'shameful secret' context for this next dream. She was desperate to understand and be rid of what she had kept to herself for so long. Somehow, the family's dirty linen had to be made clean. She recounted this dream to me:

It was about being in a ladies' toilet. I was desperate to go to the toilet. I was trying to find one, and it took me ages. I seemed to be going up and down stairs - I remember my legs making that movement - but couldn't find a toilet. And when I found it and got in I knew it was a toilet because I could see the toilet pan was there and the cistern. There was no one else in there - well, there was no other woman, but there was a man's voice - someone in one of the cubicles, and he was shouting. I couldn't see him but I

recognised who it was. And I thought to myself at the time -

'Why is he in the ladies' toilet?'

And I remember that on the cistern was this bag of washing, and I thought,
'Who has left their washing here in the toilet?' Well I must have

used the toilet because as I got up, all the washing fell down the toilet.

But I couldn't walk away and leave it. I had to get the washing out.
The toilet hadn't been flushed and there were other things in the toilet. As I was trying to

get this washing out, I was feeling sick. I can't tell you what the

washing consisted of.
All I know is that the washing was white and clean,
and what stuck out when I was trying to untangle it out of the toilet pan,
was a man's black sock - one sock.

In the middle of giving me a clear explanation of her dream symbolism, she suddenly asked herself the question, 'Why did it take me so long to find the toilet? Was it because I couldn't *see* to find it?' She was exploring this part of the dream metaphorically. She had hung on to her feeling of family shame for decades, but not until now had she been able to 'see' (understand) how she might be rid of its effect on her life by dealing with it, and feeling clean. In her dream she reckoned that the lack of seeing, and then the ability to see again was to be interpreted, not literally, but metaphorically.

The symbol of one sock left in the washing led her to reflect on her broken marriage relationship. She knew her husband had a leg amputated some years after he left her.

Hearing impairment

Dreams can help to confront denial

During the years when I had a hearing aid but rarely wore it, I would find myself in situations where I could not follow a conversation and had to remain either in ignorance of what was being said, or admit to having my impairment and ask the speakers to repeat what they had said. I was in denial about the extent of my impairment. My dream team on the other hand was not, and persisted in sending me dreams where I could not hear what was being said! It was a worrying aspect of my life because hearing accurately was crucial to my work with people, and worry triggered those dreams until I wore my hearing aid more regularly.

ADRIENNE'S DREAMS

Adrienne is a vivacious woman, who became completely deafened in her adult life. She offered me vivid current dreams and here are two, each very different from the other.

The first was scary and threatening, and yet when she interpreted it, felt reassuring. In the dream a missile tore a hole through the place she was staying with her young children, but she protected them and managed to cope well in the situation. Some years before, she had divorced an abusive husband, and at the time of the dream unresolved financial business from the past meant that he (the missile symbol in her dream) was intruding destructively again into their lives. In this dream her impairment was not an issue, and she said of it 'I can hear well in this dream. I can hear the missile and the wind, the children talking and laughing. I am not deaf. There is no disruption in communication. I am aware of sight, sound, taste, touch and smell.' The dream was not about her disability, it was about her ability to cope well in this current threatening situation.

At the time of the second dream, a relationship with a male friend - a potential new partner - had recently ended. It is a fairly typical reaction to a significant loss that Adrienne's thinking about the relationship and attempts to understand its breakdown continued for a time after the actual parting, both in waking and in dreaming.

Years before, Adrienne had enjoyed learning Latin American dance, and the creativity of her internal dream team thought up a new dance title around which to weave the dream plot and catch her attention. In this dream she was fully aware of her hearing impairment, but also of the triumph of her ability to dance to rhythm in spite of being deafened. In the dream, however, her friend makes no attempt to understand her communication about her continuing ability to enjoy life. He appears to be on a different emotional wavelength. Then, as if to emphasise both her impairment and its challenge in communicating effectively in this relationship, her mobile phone with its built-in software specific to her hearing needs, rings, potentially interrupting the communication they do have at this point. She has been keeping it hidden - tucked away beneath her foot under the table! Here is part of her dream record:

I want to leave, and encourage my male friend to leave with me holding his hand. There is music playing a sort of Salsa/Latin American type beat.

There is a dance to it, which has a name "La Incaga".

I am dancing and jiggling by his side. My body is so close to his.

We are now on a packed Mediterranean beach, it is sunny and warm. He is dressed in his jacket and trousers and shiny shoes, which are all dry by now, but it is hot. I want him to see me dance, I want him to know I can dance even though he does not understand how I can dance to music if I am deaf.

But here I can hear the music and I can dance just fine. I want to impress him, please him.

The beach is packed, people are dancing in their swimming costumes; it looks such fun. I so want to join in. But I stand jiggling by his side holding his hand, my body knocking against his body as I jiggle. I am thinking, 'Surely he must feel me doing this?' But he makes no mention of how well I can dance. I want to act 'cool'. I look down at his trousers and the lower legs are still wet from the water. I want him to dance with me. Instead he suggests we sit at a table. He calls a waiter over. He asks the waiter 'could we have some information on 'La Incaga?' He is speaking in Spanish now.

He has missed the point completely. He wants to talk semantics. I am hurt and frustrated. The waiter and the waiter's father talk to each other, not understanding, and then they say 'Oh, La Incaga!' They go to get some information.

A mobile phone rings: it is under my foot; it is my mobile. (A heavy Nokia Communicator). I keep my foot on it, crushing it into the sand. The waiter wants a pencil, which is by my foot, so he can write down the information.

I bend down and try to pick up the pencil whilst pushing my foot down strongly on the mobile. I am irritated because it is not information that I want. I am wanting to dance and impress and please. I wake up.

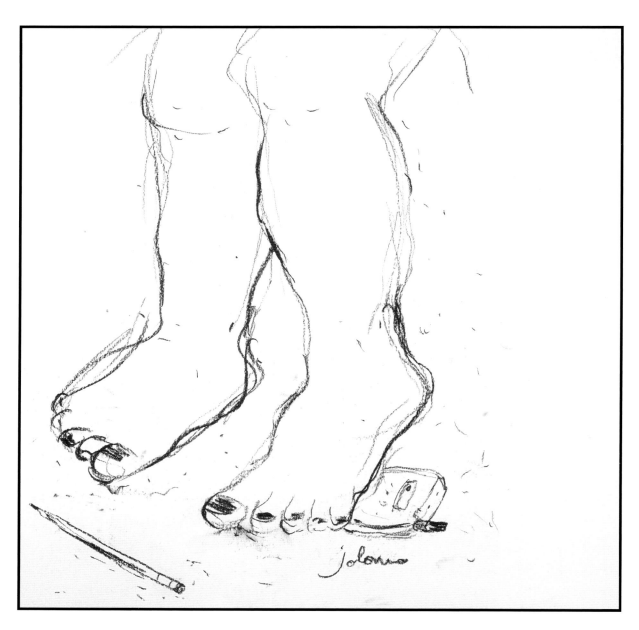

ADRIENNE'S DREAM

Angrily Adrienne pushes her foot down so strongly that she risks crushing her phone - this symbol of help in communication - into the sand. Was her dream helping her explore why her relationship had ended? Did her left-over anger about the break-up trigger the dream? This dream is about her feeling a lack of real communication with this friend. Did her male friend leave her because he could not cope with it, the avoidance the dream portrays?

Summary

Dreams with symbols linked to their impairment appeared when the dreamer was conscious of feeling disabled either emotionally or in their ability to communicate. If there is no feeling of being disabled in waking life, there seems to be no need for symbols of it in dreaming.

For personal consideration:

If you have sensory impairment, does it ever appear in your dreams?

- Do you dream that you cannot see or hear, touch, taste or smell, or that your communication is affected by your impairment? If you do, ask yourself what it means.

- How do you feel about your impairment? Does it need more attention?

- Could your not seeing, not hearing, not tasting and so on, be instead a metaphor for what is happening in your life right now?

On the other hand, your dream might include a symbol from the area of your impairment; something adapted to help you live more safely or effectively - a computer, a phone, spectacles, a smoke detector, or something you once used to help you function more easily.

- If so, what does that symbol mean in your life just now?

- What was happening to it in your dream?

- Might what was happening to it be a picture of what is happening in your life?

If you are a non-disabled person, how do you interpret dreams where you are aware you cannot see, hear, taste, smell or touch? Might these experiences be metaphors?

9. THE DREAMS OF PEOPLE WITH CONGENITALLY IMPAIRED VISION

Contrary to popular belief, people totally blind since birth[24], do dream. Their dream experience, as for all dreamers, is based on their waking experience.

Other dreaming senses

Many people assume that if a person cannot see when awake, he or she will not dream; those who depend on sight seem to forget that dreaming need not be visual. In dreams people can experience sound, silence, rhythm, smell, taste, touch, body movement, falling, flying, spatial awareness, wind blowing through our hair, rain falling on our cheeks, plus that odd awareness of 'just knowing' in spite of the evidence of the senses to the contrary - all the countless ways information comes to people awake and with all senses available to them.

In today's world where politically correctness demands respectful language, the words 'impaired vision' are used to cover a whole range of visual experience, from a great variety of differences in sighted experience to that of never having had physical sight.

Dreaming can usually reproduce the whole range of what has been available to the dreamer in waking experience, unless that area of the brain has been impaired that contributes a particular aspect on the dreaming network. People, therefore, who are born with light perception have this capacity in their dreaming; those who are born with partial vision usually have the same partial vision in their dreaming; those who see in shades of black and white, do not dream in colour - and so on. But later in this chapter I will question an assumption some researchers have made about the dreaming capacity of those that have been 'totally blind since birth'.

The guide dog as a dream symbol

Meanwhile, I'll take up again the theme of guide dogs in the dreams of their owners. For instance, in the case of Margaret - a lady with

---

[24] I take the liberty at places in this chapter for the sake of clarity, of using a non-politically correct phrase - like 'totally blind' - to describe as accurately as I can, what I mean

a lovely sense of humour! She has been totally blind from birth, and described a very different dreaming experience to those in my study (Ch. 8) who had acquired visual impairment. She chatted with me in an anecdotal way. Her dreams have no visual component: she senses as she experiences in waking life, and expresses her own delightful way of relating to the world - with a huge enjoyment of food, and a fear of all things electrical. She has a talking clock, but in her dreams it communicates to her more than just the time of day!

She now has her fifth guide dog, and was eager to relate that her dogs have come regularly into her dreams over the years. She worries about her dogs, and believes that is why she dreams of them so often. Apparently she talks constantly to any current dog in their waking life together, but in her dreams they talk back to her! In dreams, she recognises each dog's voice; all her male dogs have had deep masculine voices. Her first dog was small and frisky, and she heard her speak with an Irish accent!

At one point she began to worry for some reason, that her current guide dog did not really enjoy what he had to do for her each day. Her anxiety produced a dream in which he slipped away from her in the street and with the gruff words 'Oh to hell with this! I've had enough, I'm off!' left her helpless to follow him, stranded, an empty harness dangling from her hand. With a previous dog she recalled being concerned because he had sustained a leg injury. In a dream when she wanted him to board a bus ahead of her he did so obediently, but she clearly heard him mutter 'You know, this is going to hurt me'. Each of her dogs symbolised her dependence on them for her freedom to move, and her safety whilst travelling; and there was much at risk for her should they prove not to be content in their work, or should their injuries make them unable to take her where she needed to go.

But let me relate also some of the fuller accounts I documented during my studies.

DAVID'S DREAM (i)

David's mother contracted German measles in the first few months of her pregnancy, and as a result he was born blind. Over the years of his adult life has had a series of guide dogs that became very much part of his everyday life and experience. So much were they a part of my experience of David's body image, that I somehow imagined they would be there guiding him through his dreams. But this was not the case: his dream team had other ideas!

Here is a dream extract from a time in David's life when he felt he was getting nowhere, and needed help.

I wandered through **corridors** with a fence on either side of me.

And I seemed to walk for a good two or three hours anyway, not doing much, but just walking. And I came into one passage and I was met by an animal:

a very, very large animal that looked like a cat,

and it meowed like a cat, but it behaved very oddly.

I heard the cat meow so I put out my hand to stroke it,

but he sort of spat and hissed at me, and turned his back

and let me hold his tail. And at this stage he led me down, oh for quite a long time, through some other corridors, holding his tail. And every time I put out my hand to stroke him, **he wouldn't let me**,

but he let me hold his tail.

'That's unusual for a cat', he commented in the course of describing his dream, 'because cats don't like you touching their tails. But this was a very large - I mean on his four paws he was about as tall as I was - so I could easily hold his tail, and it was about the height to be held quite happily. And after that he left me.'
David explained that in the dream the cat backed into the very same position at his side as his guide dogs had been trained to do, so that he felt secure.

'Why should you dream of a cat, and not of your own guide dog?' I queried. He laughed: 'I've always liked cats better. I was saying to a friend only last week that I wish they could be trained to guide me!' As we further teased out the meaning of the cat in his dream, David told me that it had appeared just when he was feeling alone and rather frightened. With the cat he felt confident in spite of it not wanting to be petted. David is employed by the church, and being led by this very special, mysterious animal and gaining new confidence through its company reminded him of Psalm 23 in the Bible where God the shepherd leads his trusting sheep through difficult places.

Out of seven current dreams David gave me, there was one where a dog was 'wandering around, and didn't seem to belong to anyone'. This dream was experienced shortly before the 'big cat' dream. It is likely that the wandering dog was a symbol of the way David was feeling around that time: the whole dream theme was about wandering, there was no significant happening or interaction. But another was a nightmare - one that related directly to a very recent and real traumatic event:

The waking trauma

David with Ramsey his guide dog, headed off to a local wood ten minutes' walk from their home, where as usual he released him from his harness to give him freedom to play by himself. But after a while Ramsey returned, whimpering. David ran his hands over his dog's body to diagnose the cause and felt warm blood running from a paw. At once they headed home, where Ramsey refused to go in, but lay on the doorstep while David phoned for help.

A friend responded immediately, but when he arrived to take Ramsey to the vet the dog, weak from loss of blood, did not want to move. Eventually, with great care and gentleness they persuaded him into the car, and drove slowly lest any movement cause further discomfort. Broken glass had cut through both an artery and a tendon, and Ramsey might have bled to death. He was in care for three months before being allowed back on duty.

The traumatic dream

There was only one difference between this real incident and David's subsequent nightmare where he relived the trauma in vivid detail - a difference in speed. In the nightmare, his driver friend managed to get Ramsey into the car quickly and they raced him to the vet. This fits Hartman's[25] description of post-traumatic stress nightmares where encapsulated memories of a traumatic incident appear in waking experience as flashbacks or in dreams where the incident is re-lived, often with just one significant aspect changed.

Can 'blind' people 'see' in dreams?

I have known David over many years, but when I approached him about taking part in my studies on dreaming, and the necessary contract was drawn up and signed between us, he threw out a challenge that took me totally by surprise. 'I'm really happy to do this, Jean, because I'm hoping you'll be able to tell me that I see in my dreams'!

We were both attending a conference at the time, and another session was about to begin, so I had an hour or so to try to digest this

[25] Hartman 1996

remark, and recover from its shock, before we could discuss it. I had read several articles on the dreaming of people with visual impairment, and knew that it was widely acknowledged in dream research that people born blind couldn't see in their dreams[26]. That made sense to me; how could it be possible to produce a dream without it being based on some kind of waking experience? I recalled one article[27] where researchers owned confusion on this topic, but had assumed this could be explained away by the fact that visually impaired people use sighted language. Their research was carried out in various locations in North America where assistants gathered together dream reports from people who were blind since birth, and sent these to the main group of researchers for analysis. Those involved in the analysis had no direct contact with the dreamers, so had no way of checking with them whether or not their sighted language was an indication of an experience of seeing in a dream, or their choice of language to describe their dream story.

Later I caught up with David, and we discussed his expectations and my limitations. I checked out that the way I had invited him to take part in the research had not misled him in any way. He assured me that this subject was something he had wondered about for some time now, and welcomed the opportunity to discuss with me as fully as I wanted, and the dreams he might share with me. I said it would be impossible for me to tell him if he was seeing in his dreams. I would listen to what he told me, ask searching questions and rely on our joint ability to check on what the language he used actually meant… but even then, how could we really know? There is a popular belief to the effect that people see in dreams excerpts from the experience of former lives. I was not qualified to comment on that. Perhaps some day scientists will have the ability to televise dreams as they are happening while the dreamer sleeps? Quite a thought! An impossible task right now, but that caught my imagination.

[26] Hurovitz et al., 1999
[27] Matlock, 1988; Matlock and Sweetser, 1989; Sweetser, 1990

DAVID'S DREAM (ii)

David described to me seven dreams, the day after dreaming them, over the following months. Five had no visual aspects, but in two he reported visual episodes. During his dream of the big cat that led him through corridors he noticed that there were patterned tiles in one corridor, too far away but also so hot that they would have been impossible for him to touch and to discover their patterns from that sense. The rest of that dream was non-visual.

The other was much more visual in his experience. I report it as David told it to me.

The dream, I think, takes us back to the sixteenth or seventeeth century. It was weird! In a town or city, I don't know which, but it definitely had a square. I'd been walking quite some time to this city. When I arrived I saw quite a number of people assembled in the square, but I didn't know why, and the folk were milling around talking to each other, but they were speaking English, so it was either an English-speaking area, or in our own country, but that wasn't clear. I kept wondering why there was a big crowd in the square. They kept saying to me, 'We're waiting for the execution.' So I kept asking people who was being executed, and what had they done. Well, they wouldn't tell me who it was, and they certainly wouldn't tell me what he or she had done. All the people I kept asking were saying, 'Oh, I can't possibly talk about it!' And I didn't know what whoever it was had done, and I seemed to spend quite a lot of time chatting to different people, trying to find out, and nobody would tell me. Whether it was public knowledge, but not to me, I don't know.

I was waiting around, and then the executioner whom I didn't recognise came on the scaffold. But then the prisoner came on and it was a friend of mine who's actually my lawyer, a chap called Mike! And I was absolutely horrified to find Mike on the scaffold, for something I didn't know he had done, or not done, or whatever, but nobody seemed to tell me. And I don't know whether he was executed, for I woke up at that point.

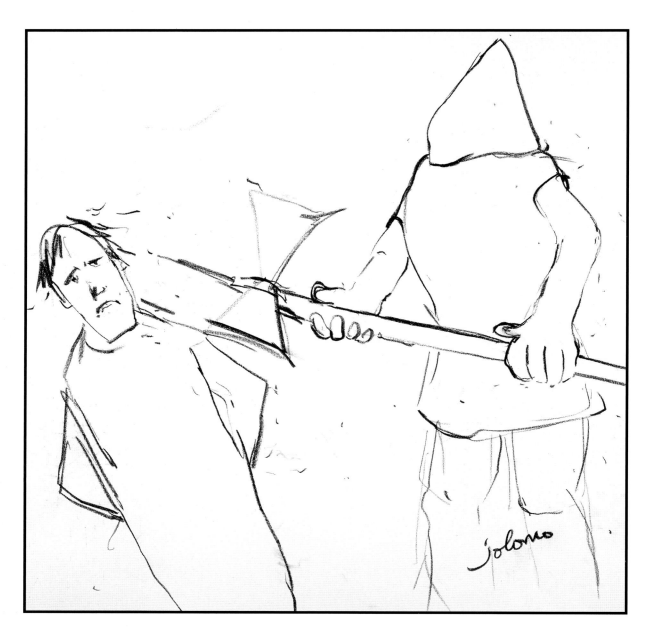

DAVID'S DREAM

When I asked David for clarification about some aspects of this dream, I checked out with him if, when he reported 'I *saw* quite a number of people assembled in the square', this was a visual aspect in his dream. He replied that it wasn't - he had walked amongst them and been aware of their bodies and their voices.

Here is a transcript extract of a conversation where we focussed on the apparently visual aspects of the dream:

'You said you didn't recognise the executioner.'

'Right.'

'Can you describe to me what the executioner looked like?'

'He was about kind of… em… a fairly big chap, broad-shouldered…em…I didn't hear his voice - I wasn't near enough to do that… em… He was wearing a sort of all-over gown. I mean, if he was wearing something underneath, I wouldn't know. He was wearing a sort of, kind of robe with long sleeves.'

'Yes.'

'And I remember looking at his hands and thinking they were big hands. I remember thinking he had great big hands, although I only saw one of them - that the axe was in - it looked a huge hand from where I was standing in the square, and that's what made me think, "Mm… he's got big hands!"'

'Uhuh … go on.'

'I couldn't have put an age on him, but I think if you were going to be an executioner you'd have to be fairly fit, and fairly young.'

'I would imagine so, yes… but that's an amazing picture you've just given!'

'What I also do remember was he didn't… he was quite… the Scots phrase is 'dour-faced': he didn't smile. He was clearly, you know, quite intent about the business he was carrying out. Whether he didn't want to do the job or not, I don't know. But he certainly made no attempt to… he didn't look straight at the crowd. He noticed the crowd there… whether he noticed the noise?… but he very briefly looked round. But I wasn't aware of him looking out to the crowd and making any reference to them at all. It was almost as if the crowd didn't really matter.'

David is a professional man in his forties, and I am confident that he reported to me a record of his experience just as accurately as any sighted person does, however his experience might be understood by sighted people.

Opinion is divided: nothing can yet be proved

I have now talked to quite a few congenitally blinded people about their dreaming and received a variety of responses to my question 'Would you say you ever see in your dreams?' Some reply indignantly, 'No! How could I see in my dreams?' Others say, 'I'm not sure.' One woman, Janet, responded immediately, 'Well, you know, you visualise if you're blind.' One remarked to me, 'If you lose your way you're far safer with a blind person in the dark or a fog, than with a sighted one. We make maps in our head, based on past experience. We don't rely on visual clues in the environment to find our way around, we carry the map in our mind.'

How does a child born totally blind in a sighted world make sense of what people describe? She stores in her mind working constructs that make sense to her at the time, and as she grows older she refines these to bring them in line with her rapidly expanding personal experience. She smiles, or she scowls and her parents might tell her she has a lovely happy smile or say 'Wipe that scowl off your face!' She connects that information with what she is feeling and her sense of what is happening in her own face. She hears the voice of someone she knows, and begins to discern whether that person is smiling or scowling, and how they may be feeling. She learns to read, and suddenly has access to a world peopled with folk she will never meet, in scenery and with experiences she has never had described to her previously. Again, she stores in her imagination some construct of their world - what they wear, how their appearance is described, what they do, how they feel. Anything stored in a person's waking memory should be available for their use in a dream, together with the wealth of associations and connections made between their own waking life and the mental existence of each symbol.

28 Hurovitz et al: 1999

One team of dream researchers[28] in America, trying to figure out whether or not congenitally blinded people really could see in their dreams, wrote: 'As Kerr (1993) notes, terms or phrases that seem visual in dream reports from blind subjects may represent spatial constructions that do not require visual imagery.'

David's brain has some mechanism that is activated when he hears a description of a facial expression because he can link it to sensations in his own musculature during times of similar emotion. He has learned and stored it somewhere in his mind, and has access to such personal constructs in his dreams. If he does not name this different way for him of sensing, 'visual', what name should he give it? He has learned it from the seeing world. Nobody can prove that his 'picture' is what sighted people see. But nobody can prove that one sighted person sees exactly what another sighted person sees! In occasional dreams, something different from his usual way of experiencing the world happens for David: he connects to the kind of experience that as far as he knows, sighted people speak of as 'seeing'.

I am a sighted person, and when David described those dreams to me, I could visualise them. If you are sighted, you will be able to see in the illustration of David's dream what Jolomo visualised as he read David's dream. Is this the picture you saw as you read about David's dream? Perhaps it's not. We cannot know precisely what another person sees. A dreamer like David may give a different weighting to what he experiences as being visual as opposed to material linked to other senses. If so, this may be explored with him.

Summary

If you have the privilege of listening to a dream of someone born with total visual impairment, don't be side-tracked (whether you are sighted or not) into wondering whether what she has seen in a dream is what you would have experienced if you had had that dream. If she wants you to help her understand it, then go ahead - ask the questions you would ask if you knew the dreamer had perfect vision.

The dreams of a person with visual impairment are just as full of symbolism and metaphor as those of a sighted person, and whether or not they see in their dreams is another question that as yet has no definitive answer. It appears that some people totally blind from birth do have an experience in their dreams similar to what sighted people would call 'visual'.

REFLECTION

You might like to try this:

If you want practice in selecting questions to help someone interpret their dream, you might like to design a few for David's big cat or execution dreams[29].

I would suggest that one way to do that would be to read through the dream and underline, or in some other way that suits you better, make a recorded list[30] of all the symbols and metaphors you can spot there:

> e.g. symbols: corridors, fence…
> metaphors: 'I was walking for hours', 'the cat spat and hissed at me…'

When that is finished, design some questions you might ask David to help him explore the meaning he associates with each one:

> e.g. 'What did wandering alone along those corridors feel like for you?' Give him time to think and reply, then ask, 'What do these corridors symbolise for you, David?'

---

[29] David's nightmare dream of his dog's accident is a different kind of dream, since it re-lives a real incident and comes as a heightened memory package. In such a dream, only what is different from the memory of the incident is likely to be symbolic. This dream was unpleasant, but it did not lead on to even more frightening nightmares around the original incident that might be a sign of post-traumatic stress, and an indication of the need for professional help.

[30] Again this is suggested in Appendix 1

Or :

> 'You implied that this big cat symbolised God for you, David. What do you make of the part in your dream where the cat spat and hissed at you?'

When you do this with a person to help him or her understand their dream, only stay with a question as long it seems to hold the dreamer's interest, then move on. If the dreamer says something like 'I've no idea', it could be appropriate to respond, ' You might want to think more about that when you're by yourself.' Give the dreamer the space he or she needs for whatever reason.

Alternatively, you might ask the dreamer to select which of the persons or things in the dream holds a particular significance for them, and ask questions around these.

But before you try it out on another dreamer, test this method on some of your own dreams.

A DISABLED DREAMING SELF-IMAGE, OR ONE THAT FUNCTIONS IN AN UNUSUAL WAY

Often there is no sign of impairment in the dreaming self-image of disabled people, but sometimes the dreaming self-image appears to be disabled, is impaired or functions in a way that seems uncharacteristic for that person. This is also a relatively common feature in the dreams of non-disabled people.

Where physical symptoms may be symbolic

Feeling trapped

Vevey (see ch. 6) had a dream where she was travelling on the upper deck of a bus. When she wished to go downstairs, she found her legs were trapped: she couldn't move.

In yet another dream she walked freely into a stately home open to the public. Almost immediately she began to float upwards, where she became trapped in an awkward position with her neck against the high ceiling and could not move to bring herself back down to the ground. People were looking up at her, pointing her out to others, viewing her condition as some kind of spectacle. There was no wheelchair in either dream, but those dreams were around a theme of her not being able to move, feeling trapped and on show.

It's a very common experience for people keeping a record of their dreams to find the same or a similar theme cropping up in dreams dreamt around the same time - perhaps a few days apart. An obvious explanation for this is that at any given time in any person's life there is likely to be a theme running through what they are feeling about themselves, probably as a result of what is happening in their lives. One dream theory[31] claims that the majority of dreams are anxiety based, and it does seem that if dreamers are worried about something, it is likely to crop up in their dreams.

So why might Vevey have two different dreams of being physically trapped? The trigger would appear to be a concern about feeling trapped. If you were Vevey and the dreamer of those two dreams, how might you interpret them?

[31] Hobson, Pace-Schott & Stickgold, 2000

Might you say something like 'Well, it's obvious what these dreams are about. I am trapped in this body. Nothing I can do about it but try and get on with my life. Wish those dreams would stop. I don't need to be reminded.'?

Or might you try to interpret it symbolically, with a reflective 'What's this about? What is it in my life at the moment that is making me feel trapped, unable to move while others watch?' It maybe your physical condition that is causing your stress; but in the dream context that might symbolise something else, perhaps something happening publicly in a relationship, or in your work or studies, or just how you feel about life's opportunities for you at the moment.

The physical symbolising the psychological

With useless legs

HELEN'S DREAM

One of the people who shared her dreams with me has multiple sclerosis (MS). In her waking life Helen's legs and feet seem to her to be swollen, and either feel very heavy or as if padded thickly with cotton wool. She drives an automatic car and walks unaided, but has limited energy. She has not travelled by bus for years because she feels she does not have enough control of her balance when the bus is moving. Usually in dreams her legs and feet are non-disabled, and just as nimble as they used to be.

With some horror and fear she described her legs in two disturbing dreams, dreamt close to each other; in the first dream there were two sections. I'll quote a few sentences from each:

Dream One:
- first section: 'Driving was **hard**, and at some time the car changed to being a bus. I was standing on the back step[32],

hanging on with great difficulty.'

[32] Most modern buses in the UK no longer have this open, very vulnerable place

- second section: 'I felt as if I was on one of those moving walkways, but it was as if I were trying to walk against it. My legs would **not** work. They felt useless.'

Dream Two: 'I started to run, but my legs got heavier and heavier … I looked down at my legs and as I looked they became one with my feet - they were amorphous, useless, huge, ugly lumps of heavy blubber.'

'But why?' she asked. 'At the time of those dreams my MS wasn't troubling me. I was feeling physically well, and able.'

'So what was happening in your life around that time, then?'

She could tell me immediately. Her two closest friends were unwell - one was already in hospital, and the other waiting to be admitted to a different hospital, dozens of miles away. She had to feel well enough to look after both friends at the same time: to go between them, giving each the emotional and social support they required. The symbol of the car (where she would be driving and in control) had changed to one of a bus (of being driven and therefore not in control), and to her barely managing to hang on from a very exposed position as it moved forward.

Helen's dream body image was highlighting the main impaired area of her physical body. 'Look' it seemed to be saying to her, 'at your feet and legs. They can't help you move the way you want to in this situation. You are feeling disabled: unable to cope'. And to underline that message, their symptoms were grossly exaggerated. Seeing them, she felt useless at giving her friends the support they would need as she rushed between two hospitals.

This dream image raised feelings of repulsion and uselessness, fear, apprehension and insecurity as she faced a most physically demanding new situation in which she wanted to do so well for her friends. What her dream body image was experiencing on the bus was a metaphor of what she was feeling emotionally - she was fearful and 'hanging on with great difficulty'.

ANOTHER DREAM FROM BETH

One of Beth's dreams frightened her. She'd had a walking impairment since infancy and in her childhood her mother often threatened her by saying 'You'll end up in an institution!' It was more than 35 years since she lived with her parents, but in this dream her parents, uninvited, had come to live with her.

My parents seem to be living with me;

I've no idea how that has come about.

I seem to be living in my own house,

but my husband is nowhere to be seen. My father is saying very little

- he seems to always be in the background.

I'm sure he has lots of thoughts and feelings with regards to what is going on,

but he's not verbalising any of it. I wonder why?

Mum seems to be making all the decisions, disregarding all others involved.

She's talking about Care Homes and

the like - hospitals - for me!

I cannot see my face,

yet I know this is about me.

BETH'S DREAM

I tape-recorded our discussion about her dream, and began by checking out some details:

'You're seeing yourself in the dream, then?'

'I'm in it. It's me she's talking about. I see myself, and yet I know - and in what I've written about my dream I've underlined 'know' - this is me!'

'You can see the rest of your body?'

'Yes.'

'But not your face… And the rest of you is…?'

'Whole. Whole.'

'So in the dream you have no face?'

'Can I tell you what I think that means?'

'Please.'

'That I don't want to see it! I don't want to face it.'

Beth needed no help from me to interpret her dream symbol of her faceless body. This was one dream where the interpretation of the way the body differed from how it looked or felt in waking was purely symbolic.

At that point in Beth's life it was becoming more difficult to cope with her walking impediment. She was in constant pain. The orthopaedic specialist was offering yet another operation, and from past experience Beth felt extremely anxious about its possible outcome. Might she be left even more severely impaired? It was difficult to face up to that possibility, and the imagined long-term consequences. The non-appearance of her face was a metaphor Beth could understand immediately. Beth has a most mobile and expressive face with absolutely no sign of physical impairment in its appearance or functioning.

With a super-prosthesis

Just in case you think all my dream examples are of people going through a hard time, let me tell you about Tom. He had a full-time job that required him to be able to climb nimbly, and in his spare time loved working with learning-disabled people. Then he became ill, had a leg surgically removed, and it became impossible for him to continue in his employment. Once he grew used to his prosthetic leg he again became in involved in voluntary work with people in various charities, and then in sporting activities. One night he had a dream in which his prosthetic leg - a bit like a seven league boot - helped him move faster and more surely than the legs of everyone around him. This dream prosthesis symbolised where he now was in his life - in a leadership position with both disabled and non-disabled people in certain sporting activities. He owed this to his disability, without which he would probably have remained in his original job.

A leg - covered up - that asks too much

Fiona was involved in an accident in which one leg was severely damaged. After much time off work, she returned to employment with that leg

TOM'S DREAM

permanently impaired. Eventually her level of pain demanded more time off to rest. There was a court case about the accident in which her lawyer claimed compensation for her impairment, but it proved impossible for the court to prove which of two firms was legally responsible for the condition of the masonry that had crushed her leg, so although both had adequate insurance, neither could be made to pay. She received no compensation. She became a wheelchair user, returned to work, and then was signed off once more. She hid her pain from colleagues as long as she could. They gave her tremendous support, but eventually Fiona began to face the possibility of early retirement. Around this time she had a dream:

FIONA'S DREAM

I was in a dress shop trying on new clothes.

Just before closing time I was in a top and trousers set that I liked.

I looked at the price tag on the trousers and saw

it was £949.00!

This was far too much for me to pay!

I wondered what the staff would think of me taking up all their time, then going out without buying anything.

FIONA'S DREAM

Fiona added, 'By the way, in the dream I was tall and slim - my legs were good. I could turn and twist in front of the mirror. No sign of disability.' I asked her what she thought the dream meant. 'Those trousers were covering up my disability that has been asking too much of me. That leg has been asking too much of me - too high a price to pay.' When she interpreted the dream Fiona initially thought about the emotional and physical cost to her of the leg's pain. It wasn't until later that she realised that the money she had never received in compensation might also be part of the dream's symbolism.

And if there is no body in dreams?

Graham has a congenital condition - cerebral palsy (CP). I hadn't seen him for years, but contacted him by phone to tell him of my study. He was interested, but when I e-mailed some questions I would want to ask about his dreams if he agreed to take part, he responded, 'I would love to help you; but I'm afraid that your questions appear to have no relevance for me.' My heart sank as I read this. He continued 'When I dream my body is an amorphous presence which can somehow deal with the situations in which I find myself. The question of my disability seldom arises.'

He went on to give me what might be a clue to his neither seeing nor experiencing his body in

his dreams: 'From the age of four to late adolescence, I enacted a fantasy which allowed me to live 'normally' in an action-packed world. I did not 'escape' from CP, but adapted disabled paraphernalia to be part of my parallel world. For instance, my National Health Service tricycle was a very sophisticated form of transport… I would love to talk about these things.' And his parting shot was 'Why should I dream of running when I have never done so?'

I was fascinated. I had to know about this! I arranged to visit him to continue the conversation and have the consent form signed, should he so wish. It was a most interesting time. What could he mean by saying he was amorphous in his dreams? Was he saying just what many others experience, that sometimes his dreams do not include a symbol of himself; that sometimes he is not in his dreams? I thought perhaps there was more to his experience than that, but I was not certain. I asked him if that was what he meant.

'I do not see myself at all!' he responded with great emphasis. 'It's just taken for granted that the things I am doing in the dream are possible. Obviously if I was debating, I was debating in such a way that nobody was concerned about my speech impediment. If I was writing, no one was concerned about the slowness of my writing, and so on. But I wasn't actually doing it: these things were happening without me being conscious of it.'

I was struggling to understand. 'So would you say that in your dreams you don't have a speech impediment?'

'I don't want to answer your question because I'm not certain that I have, or have not. The fact is that what is being done in the dreams is getting done. It's generally being done in a world that is - quotes - 'normal', so that I have what is required to get the task done. So I don't actually have dreams about failure as such, or success.'

During this recorded conversation I felt myself beginning to understand, then growing convinced that I did not. I ventured, 'I'm remembering that when a person has a stroke and as a result becomes totally speech impaired, he or she still dreams of speaking as he did in the past. Is that what is happening in your dreams?'

But his answer to that was 'I think looking back on my recent career, talking publicly as I do physically, was a denial of my speech impediment. Therefore in life I was denying it - therefore in dreams it wasn't there either. I feel that I burned myself out denying all these things. And I feel much more psychologically at ease with myself since I stopped denying any of these things - since I 'came out' as a disabled person.'

Eventually I understood that Graham was giving me an example of the dreams of a person who all his life had managed through a very active and productive fantasy life to live in a way that somehow compensated him for living in a body that was seriously physically impaired. He had managed to believe that he could disregard the effects of his being a disabled person on his waking life, and this had spilled over into his dreaming life.

He rounded off that part of our conversation by saying that he thought he was still in the process of working these things through: his 'coming out' had been recent. He told me that he was beginning to acknowledge his disability, and had begun to use a wheelchair. Perhaps all this was borne out in the sequence he subsequently shared with me of four current dreams over a period of weeks. In them, his dreams were beginning to acknowledge his body:

- In the first he was watching himself walking on his knees (something he had done in childhood), but doing so along a hospital corridor as a naked adult. His attention was focussed on a particular part of his legs, but he chose not to explore with me the significance of that for him.

- In the next he was high up in scaffolding, discussing various matters with Tony Benn, the politician. Both men were amorphous in the dream: neither had a body, but the conversation was the focus of the dream, not their bodies.

- In the third dream he knew that his **carer**, living half a mile from his home, had not come to get him up and dressed that morning. He decided he had to go and fetch her. He saw himself doing this, **walking** easily, dressed in brown corduroy slacks. He then returned to his house walking alongside her. During this dream process Graham watched his body. He was not in the dream body, **not feeling** a **sensation** of walking.

- In the last dream, a crowd of men from his profession were all whizzing back and forwards at a great rate of knots, doing **business** from wheelchairs while he watched, again amorphous.

In Graham's description of what had been both in his fantasies and his dreams since childhood, the idea of his dreams compensating for disability by totally ignoring the fact that he had a body can be seen in operation. But as he began to acknowledge what he had previously denied, it was fascinating to discover that his body began gradually to appear in his dreams, symbolically representing what his dreams were processing.

Summary

I believe that all the dream symbols explored in this chapter are from dreamers who were facing major personal issues at the time, and could be described as being in a transition process. Each faced a different transition. Although there were physical components in the transition for some, for most the greater challenge was psychological, and the dreams treated this symbolically. This might indicate the dreamer's anxiety about his or her physical condition, or be interpreted as a symbol or metaphor of current psychological experience. In dream interpretation, both have to be checked out. Although this chapter has given examples only from the dreams of disabled people, the dream symbolism described here appears also in the dreams of non-disabled people.

REFLECTION

Whether or not you are a disabled person, consider:

The next time you have a dream where you are aware of your own body, how you looked and what you did, take a bit of time to recall how this was for you.

- Was there anything about your dream body different from the way it looks or functions in your waking life? If there was, describe what was different for you.

- How did that difference from your waking life feel to you in the dream?

If you think the way your body was in the dream has some significance, consider:

1 Might it be a reminder to you of something physical that is happening in your body?

2 Was it perhaps symbolic of what is happening in your waking life?

3 Might it be a compensation for something you are denying about your waking body?

4 Was the action your body was experiencing in the dream a metaphor of something currently taking place in your waking life - perhaps in a relationship?

5 Why do you think you had this dream?

11. DREAMERS PUT THEMSELVES OR OTHERS IN WHEELCHAIRS

Our dream symbols are usually people, places and things familiar to us in our everyday lives. Dream wheelchairs can appear for non-disabled people when life brings them into contact with actual wheelchairs, and their dream team adopts these as useful symbols.

An example from a novel

I was very interested to find an example of a wheelchair dream symbol in a novel[33] I read. In the story a young woman abandoned her husband, escaping from an unsatisfactory marriage. She found employment as personal assistant to a young wheelchair user. A few days into her new job she dreamt of her husband being in that wheelchair. A new factor had come into her waking life - that a person for whom she was responsible was in a wheelchair - so her dreams had a new symbol in the language they used to convey meaning to her.

A wheelchair carries an aspect of my personality

As far as I can recall I did not dream of wheelchairs until I began to work with people who were wheelchair users. While I worked in that setting, I recorded five personal wheelchair dreams. Sometimes I was the wheelchair user, sometimes it was my father (who died twenty years ago), and in another a young male stranger. The first one I dreamed really disturbed me. It was a nightmare. I recorded it on my computer:

[33] Cusk, 1997

JEAN'S DREAM

It was like a snapshot taken at a group outing, shot from just above ground level. There, close together as if just off the beach was an untidy huddle of abandoned wheelchairs, and in one right in the centre, was Dad: old, old and so frail. Looking as if he were beyond it, really. He was propped up on this wheelchair somehow, asleep or unconscious, and as I looked, his head jerked down onto his right shoulder. Had he died? His neck had no support.

I had been aware for some time, that when I dream of my father his image usually signifies the part of me in charge, the organiser, and the thinker. In our family, that is who Dad was for me: I could rely on him always to be in control.

At the time of this dream my husband was off work. His leg was in plaster following an operation to his ankle, and I was trying to care for him while coping with what seemed an over-full workload, including clients who came to our home. This dream happened after a night of typing audiotape transcripts and crawling into bed past midnight, utterly weary, muscles tight and cramped: my neck and shoulders a total ache. The dream was horrible - but it reflected very well the psychological state I had reached through stress. Trying to interpret it I began to wonder if I had killed off my ability to think straight, to organise my life, or was my dream showing me what would happen were I not more careful?

The irony of this dream for me was in its setting. My favourite way of relaxing and letting my body and spirit revive is to walk along a Scottish island machair - that strip of short sea-salted grass strewn with crushed seashells and wild flowers, just above a wind-blown deserted beach of white sand. That's where the wheelchairs had been abandoned, piled together, but that's where I longed to be, to shed the accumulated stress of my work with troubled people, my study of aspects of disability, and taking care of a temporarily disabled spouse!

JEAN'S DREAM

The wheelchair symbol was a vehicle to carry the part of me exhausted, and in pain - emotional and physical - no longer comfortably managing my busy life. I had been disabling myself. I chose to interpret it as a warning: 'See what could happen? Something has to give!'

Wheelchairs may symbolise disability in general

A woman who took part in my study was chairperson in an organisation set up to help people, unemployed for some time, to get back into work. She was visually impaired. In one dream she was up on stage dancing in front of several groups of people who were sitting around, watching her. In talking about her dream she recognised that each of the groups she had seen there, represented people her agency helped. Each member of one group was sitting in a wheelchair. Those wheelchair users symbolised for her disabled people, regardless of their need to actually use a wheelchair. This was like the blue and white symbol used in our society to cover the provision of facilities for people who fall under the 'disabled people' spectrum although they may or may not all be wheelchair users.

Wheelchairs may symbolise emotional or professional disability

One of my colleagues was for a time supervising the work of a non-disabled trainee counsellor working with a client in a wheelchair. The counsellor was greatly challenged by this relationship wondering if she could possible empathise with her male client's life and experience. The supervisor, anxious lest she was not giving the counsellor the help she needed, awoke one morning with a strong clear dream image in her mind: a simple picture of three empty wheelchairs. Her interpretation was that each wheelchair represented one of the persons involved: the client, the counsellor and the supervisor, because each felt in some way disabled by what was going on in this relationship triangle.

Wheelchairs may symbolise different things even in the same dream

KATHERINE'S DREAM

Katherine, a woman in her early forties, was advised by her doctor to leave the job she loved. Her older sister with cerebral palsy had been a wheelchair user since the age of thirteen. Katherine's own neurological condition was both rare and life-threatening, but a hidden disability. Most people knew her as a healthy, lively, good-looking multi-talented professional person and young mother - someone who cared for others in their difficult times. On sick leave whilst undergoing further medical tests, Katherine battled with this medical advice, with the prospect of others having to know of her condition, and with God, whom she believed had called her into the work she so enjoyed, and given her the gifts and ability to work with people in need. But to go on as she had been doing, seemed impossible. Her energy would suddenly vanish for no apparent reason, and although on some days she felt better, at other times had no feeling in her feet, her hands shook and her speech was muddled and slurred.

She had a powerful and complicated dream. As it began she was in a heavy electric wheelchair driving into a clean white building she described as a hospice. When the nurse there carefully removed her shoes, her feet had turned green - gangrenous. The nurse told her she would soon be confined to bed, and would not have long to live.

Katherine remembered different scenes in this dream. In most, but not all, she was in the wheelchair. Here are further extracts:

I am looking up the website[34] and have printed off the wrong page. It's full of Latin medical terms. My Internet site is stuck on some weird page. It has a sword on the top and I can't get out of it…

Next I am in the wheelchair driving myself into a dark cavern-type area. There is a man preparing a body to go into a casket. The body is dressed like a knight and there is an air of respect towards the deceased. He asks me if I have never heard of his order and of his church and I say no… I didn't want to join his church though there was something beautiful and mysterious about it…

Next I am not in the wheelchair, but neither am I physically with the group of people that I am watching. It's like I am out of my body.

[34] One that described her medical condition

In the final scene, not she, but another young woman was in a wheelchair and was taken in a goods lift to the light airy top floor of a building where shafts of bright sunlight streamed through skylight windows. There, as Katherine recorded, the young woman *'gets out of the chair and lies on the floor feeling the wood beneath her, touching it with her hands. She smiles and has a look of absolute peace on her face.'*

It was not an easy dream for me to receive by email. I knew of the seriousness of Katherine's neurological condition. Was this dream picturing her thoughts on what might shortly happen to her? Was it a dream triggered by her anxiety about the symptoms she was experiencing? Might the various scenes be symbolic of experiences she had been through with others in the course of her work? I could not know for her.

I responded by inviting her, since she wanted to begin to explore the meaning of her dream, to look at some questions, one of which was 'What do wheelchairs - and being in one yourself in the dream - symbolise for you?' Our e-mail conversation around the dream continued for some days, during which I was very relieved I had not attempted to interpret it on her behalf!

Here are some e-mail extracts showing how Katherine worked to understand it, and how the meaning developed for her over time:

Wheelchairs can mean lots of things for me in my life. I think in this dream it almost represented freedom and yet power. I was aware that in the dream that's what I had with it. It didn't feel cumbersome. In real life I know that these chairs are, and if I was that disabled my life wouldn't flow so smoothly and I wouldn't have as much freedom getting from A to B. Not sure. I guess it could be a symbol for disability. Though I guess I am using my disability to walk away from my present work situation. Giving me freedom. I might not feel like this in a couple of months!

I guess the wheelchair is an anchor - something to represent solidness, a grounding. At times in my life when I am working with people I do experience a similar thing. It's like an observation, a realisation, an understanding... I had wondered if this was about death and would I like it to be, but today if feels as if it is more about what I still have it within me to do. If I stay grounded then it's OK having these abilities and there is a peacefulness about it. Oh, I don't know, Jean! Death has also been on my mind since physically it's a possibility. Though I feel not that probable just now. Which is good. I am aware that as I have travelled through your questions the wheelchair has changed a bit in meaning. I can only sit with that just now.

On Wednesday I wasn't capable of doing much at all. I was totally exhausted. No doubt about it, my health is deteriorating. I can't hide from it anymore nor can I hide it. It is beginning to seriously affect my life. Originally I said the dream's about loss, but it's also about choices and beginnings.

I have also realised that the woman left her wheelchair to find complete peace. She lay on the floor feeling the wood and soaking up the atmosphere. I can clearly connect with her and sense it still. Within my own thoughts I have accepted disability, but I feel that I am moving on again and shaking it off as I have done in the past though not in the same way…

I've been working at my spirituality. Today I am not in a panic re the future. My gifts will grow as they are meant to, as I have the space and atmosphere of peace to allow them to do so.

I could have been stuck in that role which clearly takes so much out of me. I arrived at the old man in my wheelchair. A symbol of my disability. I acknowledged what he said, but clearly said no I don't want to do it anymore. Again my disability was allowing me to walk away. At the end of the dream I walk away from the disability (the wheelchair), which I have a feeling I will do once again, though with an awareness and acceptance of it.

The wheelchair in Katherine's dream, clearly suggested that she explore whether or not she considered herself now to be a disabled person. Had her useful life, as she knew it, come to an end? Might her gifts still grow, her ability still be expressed? Was there more to life for her?

The dream ending was significant. She had moved beyond being defined by her physical disability into a place of light and peace, of feeling grounded once more.

If you dream you are in a wheelchair, will this come true?

Many people imagine what might happen to themselves or others, based on past knowledge of what has happened to others. When a friend is diagnosed as having cancer, often our first reaction is that death must be imminent, although this might be far from the case.

Most people do not have the capacity to see into the future, even in dreams. I feel close enough to my Celtic heritage to believe that, occasionally, some persons do have dreams that seem to give them a glimpse into the future in ways that I cannot explain. Usually these same persons have little need to rely on dreams for this way of 'knowing'. The knowledge comes to them in various ways while they are awake. This concept is deeply embedded in part of our culture, but experienced only in the lives of certain people.

For most people who are not wheelchair users, encountering a dream wheelchair comes as a shock especially if they are seated in it, or it contains someone they know and love who is not a disabled person. One common and fearful reaction is to imagine that their dream foretells the future. Most dreams, however, that show things that would frighten us if they actually happened, can be interpreted in a symbolic way, or explained in terms of our anxiety lest something like that should happen. We now know which parts of our brain work together to produce dreams (see chapters 3 and 4), so it is wise first of all to consider a dream wheelchair as being symbolic of something happening to the dreamer now, rather than as a window looking to the future.

Summary

Finding himself or herself in a wheelchair can frighten a dreamer. The interpretation least likely for this, is that it will happen in waking life. A wheelchair may have several meanings for the dreamer, but only one or two are likely to feel right for this dream.

---

35 If you are working with another symbol, replace this word with the word for yours

REFLECTION

Consider the following:

(If any new symbol has come into your recent dreaming, adapt the questions below to fit it.) If you have a dream that features a wheelchair[35], but are not a wheelchair user, think through:

- What does a wheelchair mean to me in my life right now?

- Who was in the wheelchair and what does that person symbolise for me just now?

- Why should that person be in a wheelchair in my dream?

- Where was I in the dream, and how did I relate to the wheelchair or its occupant?

- Is that a metaphor of how I am relating to something/someone in my waking life now (perhaps not a wheelchair user)?

- What happened to the wheelchair in the dream?

- Is that a picture of something happening in my life just now?

- Was there anything unusual about the wheelchair in my dream? If so, what might that symbolise for me at the moment?

---

[35] If you are working with another symbol, replace this word with the word for yours

12. OTHERS DREAMING OF THOSE KNOWN TO BE DISABLED PEOPLE

When people dream of those they know to be disabled people, the dreams often portray these with non-disabled bodies.

Another angle on the non-disabled body image in dreams

Since the original group of disabled people who supplied dreams for my study were all learning to be counsellors and to be able to help other people with dreams, many of them became not only extremely aware of their own dreams but began to chat about dreaming to their friends and relatives. One of them informed me that when her personal assistants dream of her, they do not see her in her wheelchair.

This was a new angle for me on the dreaming phenomenon of a non-disabled body image. Not only did disabled people dream of having non-disabled bodies, but also others who dreamed of them had a similar experience! I felt already fully-stretched in studying the dreams of disabled people, but this information opened a new file in my mind, and soon it was far from empty!

In casual conversations with the spouses of disabled people I would ask if, when he or she dreamed of their spouse, the spouse had a dream body image that was disabled or non-disabled. Many had not thought about it, but a few subsequently monitored this in new dreams and discovered their dream body image of their spouse to be a non-disabled one.

In a research journal article[36] a brief summary of a dream dreamt by a paralysed man caught my eye: *'At a swimming meet for paraplegics. Yet all paraplegics are walking around. Not in chairs.'*

So, this same non-disabled image of disabled people appeared also in the dreams of disabled people!

I found one complete journal article[37] on the subject. A research project had been set up 'to learn about the effects of a disabled sibling upon other children in the family', and one

[36] Ryan, 1961
[37] Wunder, 1993

category that emerged from interviews was
'Dreams and daydreams about the disabled
sister or brother.' The young people told the
researcher about their dreams, but rarely
offered her any interpretation. Thus it was left
to that researcher to express her opinions (I will
put these in italics) as to what might lie behind
what she was told. She wrote:

> Some… described the dream situation
> where the sibling walked or engaged
> in activities that they could not do in
> real life - *a desire to escape the reality
> of the disability*. When it was apparent
> that several people dreamed of the
> sibling being "normal", from that point
> on the respondents were specifically
> asked if the person was disabled in
> the dream. If "okay" in the dream,
> *perhaps this is a way to escape
> current reality or an expression of an
> unconscious wish - a desire that the
> sibling be "normal"*.'[38]

This article confirmed for me that this dream
phenomenon does occur. Although I was
beginning to interpret it differently, I felt I could
understand why the author held such opinions
on the reason for their occurrence. Freud's
wish-fulfilment theory of dreams probably gives
academic respectability to the fact that in
everyday English language the verb 'to dream'

is often used, not to mean that a person has
actually dreamt during sleep about the subject
under discussion, but that they have wished -
often against all hope - that life was different.

Spatial relationship in dreams

The disabled counsellors I trained sometimes
appeared in my dreams, and in each there was
no sign of their disability. What seemed to be
significant for the dream's interpretation was
not whether or not their body in the dream
showed any sign of impairment, but rather
what was happening in the dream between me
and the other person. It was as if what was
happening between us was symbolic - like a
picture or metaphor of the relationship I had
with them in waking life.

Daisy - a wheelchair user - came into my
dream as a happy pink flurry of activity,
dancing about in a sunlit conservatory! The
bright conservatory had steps going down to a
dark hotel lounge, and I was at the far side of
the lounge watching her from a shadowy
distance. In the dream I knew that the pink
flurry was Daisy, and when later I tried to
understand the meaning of the dream it
seemed to me to be an enchanting symbol of
the way she was in the training group - happy,
full of fun and femininity but sometimes very
challenging for me to pin down to working at a

[38] Wunder, 1993

more serious level! Sometimes I felt she lived on a different plane - one I couldn't reach - and the dream depicted this different level! The dream had shown me a picture of how we used the space between us: a metaphor of our relationship in the group.

In another dream I was sitting on a bus with one of the counsellors. I leaned forward precariously to observe something happening outside the bus, while he held me by the hand so I would not fall. When I tried to straighten up, I discovered there was no room left on the seat for me. My attempt to understand the meaning of this dream led me again to think of how I experienced him in the training group - and that dream showed a picture of a part of how we had related to each other. One of my main tasks in the training group is to observe what is happening amongst the trainees so I can ensure that the process is helping all members to learn. I could remember him trying to support me one day when another had aggressively challenged an observation I had made. I felt he had usurped my place by not letting me handle this, but I had allowed his behaviour to pass without comment, as had the rest of the group - and my dream team thought they needed to bring this omission to my attention!

Both those dreams of trainees had acted out a scenario of a relationship that was currently troubling me as their trainer, but that I had not yet discussed with them. (Such feedback is an important part of training counsellors: they have to learn how other people see them.) Both are very able; people for whom I have a healthy respect. I know each to be a disabled person, but when I think of them in waking I think of their personalities, of the way they relate to others, of how best I can nurture their gifts as their trainer, and not of their physical impairment. Since my dream image of each is a symbolic representation, why should I see disabled bodies if I do not normally relate to their disability in my waking conversations with them? They both have the ability to become competent counsellors.

MARY'S DREAM

Part of my research process was to ask all non-disabled participants to respond to a question about any significant relationships each might have with a disabled person. In completing her form, Mary forgot that one of her close work colleagues was a wheelchair user. Later she remembered and noted on the form that this had happened, and that she felt guilty about forgetting her. In one of Mary's reported dreams, this colleague, Senga, was a main character. Here is the dream:

I was **returning** from somewhere and I was excited.

I saw Senga standing by a wire fence and I knew she was there to meet me.

I acknowledged her, but then turned away and went to **my children** to hug them,

so I quickly forgot her. I remember hugging them in my arms, spending

some time with them. Only after that did I go up to Senga and I think I knew then that

she was upset. I realised I had **slighted** her.

Now, in the dream - only now -
was I aware what an effort she had made to get there.

So only when I went over to her did I realise she had made the journey **without** her

husband. And I realised what a huge effort she had made and how

excited she must have been standing at the wire fence,

expecting far more from me, seeing her there.

In the dream I felt **distressed** when she told me all this, but I also felt

burdened by the **responsibility** for how I had upset her.

It almost took away all the pleasure of my returning.

She wasn't just upset, like sad, she was angry.

And I was aware that I was finding it very **difficult** to tolerate her anger.

So Mary had forgotten about Senga when she filled in her questionnaire - and in this dream, she forgot again and left her standing alone. Her dream feeling reaction was the same as around her omission on the questionnaire: guilt. When we worked together to unpack Mary's meaning from that dream, anger and guilt were woven closely together. She felt guilty because she hadn't paid enough attention to her

colleague, but she was angry that Senga had just stood there, '*clinging pathetically to the wire fence*' until she caught her attention, when in the dream Senga was well able to walk over to meet her.

Mary felt that in their waking life she was left carrying all the burden of responsibility for making their working relationship good, plus

MARY'S DREAM

the guilt of knowing this was not a healthy way to be with her colleague, a disabled person. Angrily she concluded that as far as she was concerned, if her colleague wanted to have a closer relationship with her, it was up to her to make the next move. Once again, the interaction between the characters in the dream had been a metaphor using a spatial image to depict the part of their relationship that was the cause for anxiety in the mind of the dreamer.

People in our dreams can be aspects of ourselves

So far I've said very little about people in our dreams being symbols of different aspects of ourselves: my dream of my father in a wheelchair (p.93) was one such. Sometimes when we dream of people we know to be disabled, we are dreaming not about their waking reality, but about aspects of ourselves. Here is another dream of Katherine's (the person facing the possibility of giving up work, with a sister with cerebral palsy who neither walks nor speaks):

There were three of us walking in the open countryside, and I seemed very much in charge. We had to get somewhere very quickly. My sister was walking with a slow awkward gait, and lagging behind.

The third person was a woman I didn't know, and I don't remember what she looked like. She didn't interact with my sister, and always stayed with me.

She turned to me, looked at her watch, and said

'We're never going to make it!' I sighed, and thought about where we were going, trying to work out a quicker way, but knew as I mentioned it that it would require even more effort from us. She nodded, and made to move forward with me.

Just then my sister said 'Katherine' but her voice was slurred and slow.

I looked at her and inside I felt embarrassed by her, then I noticed her face and understood that she just couldn't possibly achieve the walk I had proposed.

The third person had an air of disgust about her, glared at my sister then looked at me as if telling me I was to keep going. I looked again at my sister and shook my head at the third person. I went over and stood beside my sister and said to her, 'It's OK'.

When Katherine began to interpret her dream she noted that her sister in the dream was both walking and speaking. Her wheelchair was not present. The strange fact about her manner of talking was that it was the way Katherine herself now talks if she is exhausted or under stress. Katherine guessed that the dream symbol of her sister was an aspect of herself, depicting her own impediment.

She also noticed that in the dream she was both embarrassed by her sister's condition and yet understanding of it. When Katherine had been much younger, although she dearly loved her, this was sometimes how she felt about having a sister who was so disabled. Now, becoming more and more aware of her own increasing impairment in both speaking and depleted energy levels, this was how she felt about her own disability - embarrassed, and yet understanding of what was happening to her.

And the third woman in her dream? Katherine very quickly identified that the way that woman related to the sister in the dream with disgust, anger and impatience, was another aspect of how she was relating to her own disability. She so wanted to be able to hurry on with her life, even if more effort was required to get there than she had needed before. She had been allowing the aspect of her personality that rejected her feeling disabled to accompany her, rather than to slow down and go at a pace she was more able to sustain. The interaction of the dream characters reflected the present internal conversation and struggle Katherine was having with different parts of her personality.

The dream ended with her still in charge, but choosing to reject the demands of the angry impatient aspect of her personality and identify with the aspect shown by her dream sister, acknowledging her own need to love herself with her own impairment.

A dream with a mix of disabled and non-disabled images

Dot was a young mother who after her children were old enough, decided to retrain for another profession. She had originally been involved in dance drama, but now wanted closer involvement with people in need. She was sent on placement to a centre for frail elderly people, and in the course of her training had this dream:

I saw a group of **frail** people with sticks and zimmers, all awake, all alert. They were fully dressed, talking with one another.

Children, whom I took to be grandchildren, were **rehearsing** a dance to pop music in one part of the room. In another, an old man had fallen and two staff in **pink** were attending to him. He was being sick. He was wearing **old-fashioned** blue striped pyjamas with a drawstring waist. They couldn't get him to lie down.

It was **multi-coloured** all around. Little groups were forming in rows or circles. Some were visitors. There was a lot of **laughter** and tears.

It was **dark** outside but all the lights were on. It was like a 'danse macabre'. I was looking in on them. But sister said it was the best time to come.

In a beautiful way the dream wove together images from her rounded experience - of children, in dance, and now with frail elderly people! In the dream the elderly people mostly looked very different from the way she had seen them in real life when 'many looked drugged, asleep, "not with it"', and although some were still ill and frail, others were responding to her ability by dancing with their zimmers and sticks! In her waking experience she had thought there 'were some people I could help - but some I couldn't', and her dream reflected that in a picture where some had taken on a new lease of life while others remained actively ill. She interpreted the elderly ill man in his pyjamas as an aspect of herself that felt helpless and sick when she saw how needy some people were. She needed help from those more experienced - the staff in the dream.

In her actual placement, the sister in charge of the elderly people had been positive about her contribution there, but her supervisor, an abrasive older man who had not actually seen her in that context, had not. She felt he didn't fully understand, and the dream reinforced this opinion by showing her a picture of her known abilities and with words of encouragement from the sister, her boss in the placement.

Another dream dialogue between parts of the self

Gordon, a non-disabled man, has a colleague with a son of nine years who is autistic. He rarely thinks of him, so was surprised he featured in this dream. In the past, when Gordon has played his guitar, the boy would run across the room and reach out to it as if he wanted to make that sound for himself. He has never spoken, but responds positively to music.

....

In the dream, the boy's mother was asleep and her son was a baby

- a lovely little boy.

Gordon put his hand gently and lovingly around the baby's head

and held him so that they faced each other. The baby began to grow, and as he did, he responded to Gordon to the extent that the little one began,

quite naturally, to talk with him.

....

At the time of this dream, Gordon was experiencing a new lease of life. Singing lessons were releasing his potential to communicate. Interpreting the dream, Gordon felt he was both the little boy and the one holding, facing and talking with him. Gordon had kept his ability to sing well disabled, silent. Now he was communicating with this growing part of himself that was being lovingly encouraged to have a voice. His dream reinforced and celebrated that!

Summary

When people dream of disabled people they know, they usually see or hear them as non-disabled people. This may be symbolic of the way they feel about them when awake. The interaction between the body of the dreamer and that of the other person is likely to be a metaphor of their current waking life relationship.

Alternatively, the dream character may be an aspect of the dreamer's self, and the interaction between them symbolic of how the dreamer is relating to him or herself.

REFLECTION

Consider carefully these possibilities:

Often dreams raise issues in our lives to which we are not paying enough attention. In your reflection on such dreams, look first at what is happening in your dream - what you are doing, and what is happening between you and the others, and how you feel about it. Then consider either:

- If you know one dream character to be a disabled person but their impairment is not present in the dream, is the way you are interacting there a symbolic picture of what has been happening between you in waking life?

- If so, then why is your dream bringing this to your attention just now?

or

- Could the other person/s in the dream be aspects of your own personality?

- What was your emotional reaction to that person in the dream? Do you sometimes feel that way about yourself?

- Is there an aspect of you feeling disabled or recently enabled in your life at the moment?

- Why might your dream want you to pay attention to this?

Many dreams have people in them apart from the dreamer's self, whether or not they are disabled people in waking life. Consider all people, in any dream you have, to be symbols. You may recognise them to be people you know or have known in waking life.

If you recognise them, there are three useful dream meanings for you to explore:

1. What do I associate with that person? Why should my dream remind me of what I associate with that person, or of their attributes, or of my emotional response to them right now?

2. Could this person in my dream represent an aspect of my own personality that seems important in my life just now? If so, how do I feel about it?

3. What was happening in the dream between that person and me? Is that a metaphor of what happens in our waking relationship, or of how I am treating myself these days?

Then ask yourself:

- Is there something I should do because of my interpretation of this dream?

13. WHEN DREAMERS ARE AWARE OF THEIR IMPAIRMENT

Occasionally in a dream, disabled people will be as aware of their impairment as they usually are when awake.

Mostly when dreamers are disabled people, they appear not to be aware in the dream of their motor or sensory impairment. Their dream bodies are whole and functioning well and freely, as are the senses they have available to them in waking. Every so often, however, I came across reported dreams where the dreamer was aware of the impairment, and sometimes would remark on it to others in their dream.

Two wheelchair users, both with very different physical conditions during their waking lives, went through a spell of having dreams where they walked freely, but informed complete strangers that they weren't really able to walk unaided, and usually needed to use a wheelchair. Other people with mobility impairment would walk unaided in their dreams, but describe themselves as feeling very tired and wondering if they had the energy to reach their destination: some felt that one leg in a dream would drag behind the other as they walked. There were occasions when a

dreamer had a wheelchair in his or her dream, but when recounting the dream would say to me: 'By the way, the chair in my dream was my old wheelchair, not my current one.'

Two of the men in my research reported what seemed to me very similar dreams of enjoying a wild and very physical game of rugby. Both had been keen rugby players before acquiring their impairment. In these dreams they had a wonderful time, playing incredibly skilful and enjoyable games full of bodily contact, but each had a similar experience of suddenly stopping mid-field and saying 'but I shouldn't be able to do this. I'm disabled!'

As I illustrated in chapter 8, people who are now visually impaired, but who were born and lived for some years as people with good vision, often still have very visual dreams. When I first asked one woman if she would agree to participate in my research, she smiled widely, then giggled. 'I'll give you one of my dreams I can remember right now! ' she offered. 'I think you'll enjoy it.' Out poured a dream story of how one night in her dreams she drove her friend's mini-car - stopping at traffic lights, steering around corners - even doing a right-hand turn on a street full of heavy traffic! She heard the heavy traffic on the busy roads, and as she drove she laughed and said to herself, 'My friend must be crazy to trust me to drive!' because she knew she couldn't see where she was going! It was also an unusual dream for her because in it, she had no sight, and usually in her dreams she sees vividly. Although she couldn't recall what had been happening in her life at the time of that dream, I wouldn't be at all surprised if it was dreamt at a time in her life when she metaphorically 'couldn't see where she was heading' although she was driving herself on at a crazy - but enjoyable - pace!

As with the last dream reported, people would often tell me such dreams some time after they dreamed them. They considered them curiosities, something to tell a friend or partner the following day because of their unusual nature. By the time they told them to me, they had forgotten other dream details along with any memory of what had been happening to them the day or two before that might have triggered such a dream.

Such dreams are common for all people at certain times

In fact it is quite a common occurrence for people to have a dream where they are aware that something is not as it should be. Many bereaved people have dreams where they see the deceased person alive and well, and know in the dream that this is not how it is for them in waking life. People who are divorced sometimes dream they are still married to their former spouse, and tell people in their dream that they don't understand why they are with this person because they are no longer married to him or her.

Instead of leaving that part of a dream as a curiosity, it is possible to ask the dreamer, who may perhaps be yourself when you dream like that - 'Why do you think that came into your dream? And why now?' One of my dreams might illustrate this.

I have no remaining sense of smell, having been without it for more than a decade. Only occasionally in my dreaming am I aware of a beautiful scent, an aroma or even a stench, but then, very few other people in reporting their dreams to me have mentioned smell. In a dream I had a few months ago, however, I was aware that I had lost that sense. If you have a very vivid imagination you might prefer not to read what follows!

Let me put this dream in a context. I arrived at a residential conference where I was due to give a talk on the subject of 'Dreams and Disability' the following day. Obviously I had been thinking a great deal about this subject, and had again wondered why I so rarely dreamed of having a sense of smell.

The other factor I carried in my mind at the time was a feeling of apprehension. When people discover I have been studying dreams, some expect me to be a walking dream dictionary able to produce authoritative dream interpretations on the spot! Before having the dream that night one of the younger conference members asked me some questions about repetitive dreams that were upsetting her. I couldn't give her answers about their meaning. All I could do was to offer future help if she dreamed again on the same theme, and remembered enough about what was happening in her life at that time to know what might have triggered it. That experience might well have produced the motivation for me to have my dream. She had shown me her vulnerability, and I had not been able to produce an answer to help her.

That night I had the following dream:

I was at the conference and had gone into a toilet but could not relieve myself there because it was in such a messy condition. So I reported the state of the toilet to the management. When I went back later, expecting it to be cleared, aired and freshly cleaned, it was in exactly the same state.

I had two unknown companions with me this time, standing at my side: a man about my own age with white hair, and a woman who also seemed mature. I thought they might be a married couple or two people attending the conference. I told them I would have to clear up the mess. It seemed to be my responsibility since it had not already been cleaned up, although I knew it was not my mess. They said they would stay with me while I cleared it.

The toilet pan's lid was covered with diarrhoea, and there was also a thick trail over the floor. It seemed almost impossible to avoid stepping in it, although I don't think I did. The atmosphere was close and warm, and I realised the couple beside me would be suffering because the smell must be appalling for them, although I could smell nothing. I decided to tell them I could smell nothing, so they would know it wasn't as bad for me as for them to stay there - and to give them permission to go and leave me to it.

They, however, with amazing fortitude, stayed with me, and the dream ended before I cleared up that mess.

'There might be some connection between this dream and my giving a session on dreams this afternoon', I wrote when I woke. 'This awful mess that hasn't been cleared up could represent a dream, probably a nightmare that someone has been carrying around with them that horrifies them and they don't know where they can off-load it. It could be really horrific for them, but when they let it out to me, it's not as bad for me as it feels for them. It's not my mess. I can be objective, and be part of the 'clearing up' process. I think the diarrhoea without a smell is a metaphor for the fact that other people's dreams don't usually have a negative effect on me.'

The conference I was attending was one for people in church employment, and in evening prayers the night before, the story was read of Jesus asking his friends to stay awake and support him the night before his crucifixion. Was this where my dream-producer had found the idea of the man and woman who accompanied me in the dream? Often dreams have a context of something very recently experienced - something told by a friend, read in a book, seen on TV.

There could be at least two meanings of the symbolism of the man and woman in this dream. One was that I knew many of the people, both men and women who were to listen to my talk, well enough to be certain that having them there would be a support for me, although distressing subjects might be raised. Those symbols could represent them. The other interpretation might be that the man and woman, who looked so similar in age to me, were aspects of myself that supported me in this work. Perhaps a blend of what has traditionally been thought of as 'male' objectivity (the ability to step back and figure out what is going on without becoming emotionally entangled in the situation), with 'female' intuition (the ability to hunch or sense what might be happening within another person's emotional state). Nowadays few people would think one gender has a monopoly of either! I felt reassured by the dream.

I decided to ask those attending the conference not to share their personal dreams in the public discussion after my presentation. People sometimes talk about their dreams without having reached an understanding of them, and sharing dreams in public risks feeling exposed by suddenly realising the meaning of a dream, feeling embarrassed, and not wanting to disclose more.

It's very good to share dreams with a small group of friends or supportive colleagues but probably rather unwise and unhelpful to do it where there is less chance of being well understood.

Summary

It can be fun to share a dream with others where you are aware of your disability, especially if such dreams contain entertaining absurdities, but any dream like that will be just as meaningful and full of symbolism as any other dream. It can be interpreted in the same way as any other.

REFLECTION

Suggestions to consider:

If you have a dream where you are conscious of your limitations, or of your sensory or mobility impairment, or if someone mentions such a dream to you and wants your help with it, treat it as you would any other dream.

- Try to discover what might have triggered the dream - for instance, has the dreamer been especially aware of her impairment recently?

- What is happening in the dreamer's life that might be reflected in the dream?

- Which emotions were present in the dream? Has the dreamer been feeling those emotions recently? If so, in which context?

- If there are other people in the dream including strangers, who or what might they symbolise for the dreamer?

14. MONITORING PSYCHOLOGICAL CHANGE THROUGH DREAMS

Re-reading your personal dream diary can be fascinating! In this chapter, one man's transition story of psychological change and dream imagery and its meaning unfolds over two years.

Keeping a dream diary has benefits

People who keep a diary often find it fascinating to read it through again after experiencing a time of significant change or transition, to trace how things developed for them and how their feelings changed in the process. It's very similar when a dreamer keeps a dated record of their dreams. They can see dream images and metaphors changing as weeks and months go past. Almost certainly the dreamer will be reminded of forgotten thoughts and feelings, which will suddenly make even more sense in the fresh reading than they did at the time.

Duncan, as far as I know, did not keep a dream diary as such, but because he was involved in my study, he shared some of his dreams with me over a period of time and I kept the record. He was amongst the disabled people whose body image did not immediately convey to others the appearance of impairment. Duncan is a man with what is sometimes termed

'hidden' disability. He has a spinal injury that restricts his range of movement, but for which he needs no walking aid. He also has digestive problems.

Duncan is not only confronted by his disability when he makes any movement involving his spine. He explained to me, 'I watch you in the training course bending down to pick up your bag, and I think "Ouch! She'll hurt herself!" I'm so very conscious all the time that I have to keep my body in a certain position or I'll be in pain. And I seem to project this on to others.' Duncan's mirror neurons (see p.27) were firing as he watched my movement, sending messages to his motor command headquarters dissuading him from trying that posture!

I wondered what his dreaming body image might show. Would there be any symbol of his hidden impairment? At first I saw none, but then noticed that his dream body sat still. He gave me further dreams over subsequent months, and I sensed that change in the experience of his dreaming self-image might indicate change in how he was feeling, probably not about his physical body, but more about his psychological state or identity as a disabled person.

He was training to become a counsellor and all students were expected to reflect on the experience of their own lives, past and present. They were encouraged to work on any areas of psychological growth and development that would help them to understand and feel empathy for other people, especially other disabled people, wanting to make changes in their lives. So Duncan was working on personal issues: issues that often face disabled people. He was going through a deep and lengthy process of coming to terms with some major losses in his life - some, although not all - caused by his disability. About a year after the first dream collection period, he reported having a series of dreams, similar to each other:

DUNCAN'S DREAM

In one I was playing a **vigorous** game of rugby, and in some others, was engaged in Tai Chi. In those dreams there was a **pattern**: suddenly I stopped doing what I was doing in **mid-action** because I knew that my body should not be doing this.

His waking thoughts entered his dreaming. Had his fear of sudden movement influenced his sitting without moving in the scenarios of at least two previous dreams?

I continued to mull over what Duncan had given me so far; he continued both in waking life and in dreams to process and promote his emotional, physical and psychological adjustment. He had a good capacity for reflection, and a desire for growth in self-understanding leading to a sense of integration. He knew of my interest in his dreams and his journey towards coming to terms with the disruption of his lifestyle following his spinal injury trauma.

Duncan's particular spinal injury, according to current medical knowledge, means that his impairment is likely to be permanent. At his last hospital appointment the specialist advised him not to risk an operation with a slim chance of improving his condition, but which was more likely to leave him with bladder problems and less mobility; he should accept his condition and make the best of it. So Duncan worked on strengthening his back muscles through swimming, and controlling pain through acupuncture.

I wondered why he was not yet experiencing in his dreams a freely moving self-image. I looked at the group of dreams he had given me, at their separate meanings for him, and realised that I might be observing a process towards the integration of his disability into his present lifestyle and its meaning. In the first dream offered during the six-week collection, he had expressed jealousy for those who could still be actively involved with Tai Chi and had burst into what he described as 'great racking sobs'. That dream's meaning had been obvious to him. His spinal injury had deprived him of his job - teaching Tai Chi - with all that meant to him. His next dream was a nightmare:

I was sitting at the driving wheel of my **stationary** car in the middle of nowhere, and a white mist surrounded the car. I had my young son on my lap. We could see nothing.
Without warning, the stiff corpse-like figure of an elderly stranger **injected** himself feet first and horizontally through the car door and into my side, and there was nothing I could do to stop this happening.

He awoke with his heart thumping, not sure whether his emotion was fear, terror or horror. We worked together on interpreting it, but Duncan couldn't understand its significance for him. He had a hunch that it might be about the loss of his father when he was seven, but could not see connections between his memory of his father and the symbols in the dream.

As a counsellor working with clients who tell me some of their dreams, it's been my experience that sometimes a dream that feels very significant to a person eludes understanding. I try to help them explore its meaning, but it remains a mystery. Very often if we wait days, even months, allowing it to incubate, keeping it warm by remembering it from time to time, something will shift in the client's understanding, and the meaning of the dream become clear.

DUNCAN'S DREAM

From the information Duncan had given me, I suggested that he might usefully explore through counselling the effects on his life of his father's early death, and he found a counsellor and did this. My hypothesis was that Duncan was working through a complex transitional process around cumulative loss - and that he may not yet have worked completely through it.

A few months later, responding to feedback I wrote on a training assignment where he had described working through some personal life issues, he sent me a letter that contained a dream fragment. Here is an extract from the letter:

> I have been seeing an acupuncturist/Chinese herbalist in an attempt to find a permanent solution for my stomach problem. In addition to herbs, he was going to use acupuncture for the first time yesterday, partly also for my back. In a dream, someone very heavily thumped acupuncture needles into two points on my upper chest. I had no knowledge of such acupuncture points, but on relating the dream to my acupuncturist yesterday he tells me they do exist and are called 'the points where the spirit resides in old burial grounds'. These points are only ever used when a person is stuck and unable to get over a grieving process.

So things were moving with Duncan. I decided to send him all the above collected material and ask him to talk through with me what I had written about him so far. He spent time reflecting on it, and then dialogued with me on two specific areas - the issue of his current dreams reflecting a stage in his grieving process, and new understanding he had now reached of his horrific nightmare.

He talked frankly about his stage in the grieving process around his disability. For him the dreams of being very active, and then realising he should not be moving like that, are dreams where his disability is the topic - the focus - of the dream. These dreams are illustrating where he is with it, both emotionally and physically. In waking life he swims, has acupuncture, and these are helping him move more easily and experience less pain. He realises, on the other hand, that there is little chance of his back ever being healed. He is still in a process of discovering exactly what it is he has to come to terms with. He said, 'I live with the threat of further loss and the promise of further improvement - a constant unknowing.'

Duncan told me that through his counselling process he had got in touch with the emotions and meaning of his nightmare, and now understood it. While discussing the effects of his spinal injury with his counsellor he went into an experience of incredible aloneness - feeling cut off from everyone and everything meaningful for him - an existential experience symbolised in his dream by being in his car in the middle of nowhere with nothing but white mist around him. In his dream his son was sitting on his lap, and this for Duncan was a symbol of himself as a child who had lived through the experience of the long illness and death of his father and his mother's subsequent lengthy depression. The stiff corpse-like elderly figure was the threat of the future consequences of his disability. In the dream this was being forcibly injected into his body: its feet were aimed at the precise area of lower spine of his actual injury, and he could not stop it. Duncan reached a personal understanding that this was a dream that promised him wholeness through the integration of both these major losses.

Months later I was his trainer on a module of the counselling course entitled 'Attachment and Loss'. He explained to me after it finished that he had waited throughout it, expecting that he would meet yet another unresolved and emotionally harrowing loss, but this did not happen. On the day we dealt with helping clients say goodbye to something or somebody whose loss had been painful for them, I led the group in a visualisation exercise inviting them to use it to complete a grieving process in their lives if they felt ready to do so. Duncan decided to use the experience to say goodbye to what Tai Chi had meant to him. In the visualisation he found himself standing at the top of a hill he knew well. Panting up this hill came his younger, fit self - the person he was physically before his spinal injury, sweating, puffing and blowing - and this was what he said goodbye to, instead of to his Tai Chi - and that felt great for him. He was glad he no longer needed to punish his body by running uphill!

Two weeks later he experienced and recorded another dream, and sent it to me.

I dreamt again that I was playing rugby. But this time, unlike the last in which 'my back' suddenly appeared, I played brilliantly, scored five tries and played with great determination, skill and strength. There seemed to be too many players on the field, but that didn't stop me. Also the ball was too soft - it was an old, lace-up leather version which is never seen now.

And he added, 'So in my dreams I seem to have reverted to the whole body image.'

I phoned him, wanting to know more about what he made of there being 'too many players' and the significance of the old soft ball. His explanation was that the fact of there being so many players on the field showed up how well he was actually playing - diving through tackles and leaving them to bump into each other!

'And the ball?' I asked. 'It was old and soft,' he replied, 'but somehow that allowed me to play better.' When he unpacked this statement it was to realise that although his body was now older and his muscles softer than formerly, his ability to handle and play with life had developed since his spinal injury. He now feels whole within himself in a way he never did before, and his self-image in his dreams indicates that.

The whole picture

I am fascinated by the wealth of resources - both external and internal - interwoven in this part of Duncan's life story. There was his search to regain his physical health through the medical services, awareness of the need for personal growth released through counselling training, the natural grieving processes which had become stuck moving again through counselling, Duncan's ability to be in touch with his emotions, his seeking help for both his body and spirit through a Chinese herbalist and acupuncture, and so much more in his day-to-day living that I would never hear about. Woven through it all, like a golden thread, was his dreaming process - raising issues for his attention, diagnosing, producing appropriate emotion, motivating with mystery, all monitoring the process of integration of the major losses this man had sustained over decades: a complex account of a journey towards emotional health and wholeness.

REFLECTION

In order to look back on your dreams to see if they tell an on-going story of your reactions to what has been happening in your life, you need either an exceptional memory, or a dream diary.

Your dream records hold the story of themes, emotions and show symbolic pictures of events and relationships. Mysterious symbols that you could not understand at the time of a dream might have begun to explain themselves to you in some manner. It's something that's almost impossible to do unless you've kept a record of your dreams, but if you want to follow your psychological growth and change over a period - why not try it?

You'll find guidance for this in Chapter 15 and Appendix 1.

15 WAKE UP TO YOUR DREAMS

By keeping a dream diary

It can be fascinating to launch into this venture. Those who do usually discover they have a new aspect of their lives to explore and a personal and private language of dreams entirely their own to translate into greater self-awareness and action.

It is especially helpful to have a record of your dreams when your life is going through a transition process of any kind - sad or stimulating, joyfully challenging or full of problems, dark with worry or bright with hope - a time when you are facing the unknown. Looking back over that journey can greatly increase your feelings of achievement, of wonder, of thankfulness for the support you received along the way.

Perhaps at this point you say 'But I never remember my dreams!' Unless you have sustained damage to the areas in the brain that produce your dreams, or are currently having medication that might suppress your dreaming, it is almost certain that you do dream. What might help you get into the way of

remembering some of your dreams is to make preparations to receive them. I encourage you to begin to keep a dream diary.

It requires discipline and motivation to begin and to continue, but below are some suggestions, and if you prefer an even clearer structure to follow - one that enables you easily to compare and contrast one dream's content with another - read Appendix 1.

Advance preparation

It greatly helps to plan in advance. How are you going to record your dreams? Will it be most helpful for you to have paper, a pen and a torch on your bedside table, or perhaps a new blank notebook ready for your dreams? Would you find it easier to use a small tape recorder on the spot, or do you aim to get out of bed and go to your computer carrying the dream in your memory? If you choose to tell the story of your dream to your partner while you are still in bed, or to a friend or someone who comes to help you start the day, make sure you let them know in advance so they can make the necessary preparations for recording your words and thoughts. It would be wise to ask them to treat the material you give them as confidential.

So, have everything you need ready and close at hand to begin the diary the day before you intend to make your first entry. If no grand dream comes, then record even a tiny dream snatch if you remember it; one image will do for a start! Some dreamers can get a lot from just a little dream material. You might surprise yourself. But if no dream comes, try again the next night … and so on. If you have a good imagination, why not try having a talk with your dream team about it. Perhaps they would appreciate a wake up call!

When you have a dream, record it as soon as possible

On waking, to fix it in your memory, lie with your eyes shut and recall what happened in detail.

As soon as you can after that, record it as you have planned. And before anything else, put down the date on which your dream happened. Then record it by telling the dream story as you remember it - just let it flow as if you were still experiencing it. Don't let grammar, punctuation or spelling hold you up. This is your story, for your eyes only!

Sit back, read it over, and then add details you may have missed in your haste to record it - colours, smells, shapes, sounds, tastes, body postures; its location, what was said, what people wore, especially anything you noticed that didn't make sense, or didn't seem to fit in.

One really useful thing to do if you want to and can manage it, is to make a rough sketch of any mysterious object you might have encountered, or the strange way someone was dressed, or the lay-out of the house you entered … whatever is relevant. If you heard a tune in your dream and can record this in some way, get it down before your memory of it fades.

By that time you will have on record enough for you to leave aside for a while, if necessary, and get on with whatever faces you in your life that day.

When you can make the time, sit down with the dream record

If possible, spend time later that day with your dream record. Read it through a few times. Then:

a. Give it a title

b. Note the theme or themes in the dream

c. Make a list of the emotions in the dream

d. Recall its context - what has been going on in your life that might have triggered the dream, or contributed some of the dream imagery or symbols. Make a note of your meaning for the various dream symbols, including people who appear in your dreams

e. Ponder on the activity or interaction in the dream - could this be a picture or metaphor of something that has been happening in your life?

f. Begin to record your interpretation of the whole dream, or even of part of it

And come back to it later if you can

Unless you have completely understood your dream, go back to it later, or even in a few days' time, to see if you can find more meaning in it. If you do, then record that too.

Follow the dream with action

If your dream seems to suggest that you do something, and after reflection, you think such action would be wise, then do it.

Everyone has different needs and styles in recording dreams

People keeping an ordinary diary do it as it suits them best. People telling a friend a story about an event that happened to them yesterday, do it in their own special way. Even in the way they record dreams in their diary, everyone is different. Find the way that suits you best.

Why not share it with a friend who is also keeping a dream diary?

It can be very supportive and encouraging having a friend with whom you can share the dreams you choose to tell them.

Read or send your stories to them and ask them to draw up a list of questions they would like to ask you, about your dream. You do the same for their dream.

Make an arrangement to meet, or to chat by phone or email. Work through the questions, then discuss the meanings that are starting to emerge for each of you.

Have a review and reflection time by yourself every so often

Those who take the time and trouble to make dream diaries often find it very interesting to sit down quietly somewhere by themselves, to read through their dream records for the past few months. You can see themes emerging, developing and sometimes resolving themselves, dream symbols being repeated, anxieties vanishing. You can look back and trace the stages you have grown through during a major transition period of your living. You can be amazed and awed at what your dream team has been doing while you slept!

At your review, or even long before it, adapt any suggestions of mine better to suit your own needs. If you choose to continue with your dream diary, record it and use it in a way that fits in well with your own lifestyle.

Some important things to remember:

Traumatic repetitive dreams

It is not uncommon after a traumatic experience - and sometimes months or even years after the actual trauma - for a person to have a series of nightmares that greatly trouble and scare them. If this happens to you or to a friend, it's advisable for the dreamer to seek professional help. These nightmares do not mean you are going crazy. It means that your dream team has decided that now is the time to face and attempt to resolve the effects of the trauma. It is a normal symptom of post-traumatic stress[39]. If you approach a counselling agency with this, it is perfectly acceptable that you state in advance that you are having traumatic dreams, so that you are allocated to someone trained to work in this area. Psychotherapists and private counsellors are often listed in Yellow Pages. Your doctor might advise you if you are unsure where to go for such help.

Your dreams may alter with a change in medication

I mentioned that prescribed medication might have an effect on dreams. The use of hard drugs most definitely does[40]. It's as well to remember that the brain is a chemical system: various chemicals within it help to transmit messages throughout your brain and body both in waking and in dreaming. The introduction of other chemicals to this delicately balanced system has to be carefully regulated.

For instance if a dreamer is clinically depressed, their dreams are likely to echo their waking mood and thinking processes, and that can be very scary. If anti-depressants are prescribed, their effects can be seen in dreams as well as in waking life when the medication begins to work. Some drugs can increase the number of dreams recalled, and some can produce weird, larger-than-life dream images that the dreamer might find very difficult to own and to interpret. If your dreams seem to be affected by a medication prescribed by your doctor, and this frightens you, do talk to him or her about this. This book is not designed to help you with those dreams.

Your dreams are for YOU, and spring from your mind

Remember, other people dream their own dreams. It's very rare for one individual in

---

[39] Juliette Mead (2003) has written a novel on this subject
[40] Greenfield (1997): Chapter 3 gives information about the effects of hard drugs on the human brain

western culture to dream on behalf of another. Your dreams might remind you of what you need to do for someone for whom you have responsibility or with a group to which you belong, but others have their own dreams, especially produced for them. Your dream team strives to produce the right dream for you! It can't tap into the private thoughts of your friends.

When you share dreams with a friend you may well begin to dream of that person. Think very carefully before you get on the phone and announce 'Guess what! I dreamt of you last night, and do you want a laugh? You'll never believe it!'

The people and things in your dreams are symbols, and need your considered interpretation

The question I am most frequently asked when I talk about dreams to Christian people is, 'Does God still speak to us in dreams?' In the Bible, which contains scriptures of both the Jewish and Christian faiths, there are many dreams recorded, along with the interpretations given by dreamers or those who helped them to understand the meaning of their dreams. Frequently, in those ancient records, dreams were thought to be messages from God, but to be understood as such, they were interpreted through a human mind that believed that it was possible for God to communicate in this way.

Here is an example of how I might respond to such a question posed within a private conversation. Somebody might come to me and say:

'Hearing your talk I began to wonder - does God still speak to people in dreams, or did that happen only in biblical times?'

'Let me first ask you a question. Do you believe God speaks to you when you are awake?'

'Well, yes. God speaks to me in all sorts of ways when I am awake.'

'Would you tell me about some of those ways?'

'Through my conscience, I suppose, not only in church or when I read the Bible, but when I see a programme on television about famine or earthquakes, or see a road accident, or when I hold a new-born baby in my arms, or watch a glorious sunset …'

'And how would you say you knew that it is God speaking to you at times like these?'

'Well… I suppose I believe it because of the response I have in my heart. I hope it's the way God would want me to respond.'

'So it's your personal belief that God speaks to you sometimes when you are awake - so, what do you think, when you are asleep might God speak to you in a dream?'

'It would make sense if dreaming is an extension of the thoughts and feelings we have when we are awake. That's certainly the way I interpret some of my dreams. When I have a dream like that - where I think God is telling me something - I usually feel I should do something about it. Certainly my conscience is pricked when I interpret some dreams!'

'So when you experience something in a dream you attempt to interpret it?'

'Yes. I look at the dream as being symbolic, because they always seemed to be that way in Bible stories. Do you remember that dream in the Bible[41] where an Egyptian pharaoh dreamt of seven thin cows eating seven fat cows, and Joseph was brought in to help him understand the symbolism? It was nothing to do with cows, fat or thin! What the cows were doing was a metaphor of what was going to happen in the future.'

'So you believe what you see in a dream is a picture of something else? And you've got to work out what it might mean before you get the message, if it's something God wants you to pay attention to?'

'Yes, I do. But then, there's something else. There are other dreams… well, how can I put it… where I see things that might come true. Are these messages from God?'

''Things that might come true'… Can you give me an example?'

'Last week I had a wonderfully happy dream about my friend. She had an accident a few years ago, and since then has been in a wheelchair. In this dream she was walking, almost running towards me, holding out her arms - no sign of her disability. I wondered if perhaps God was telling me that she would be healed in the future?… and if I should tell her that.'

'A happy dream for you! But why should this dream be different from others in how you interpret it? Have you wondered whether her walking freely, almost running towards you might be a metaphor, rather than taking it literally?'

'It could be symbolic? Of course… let me think… well, it's like a picture of the way we communicate with each other, really… we are moving closer together these days, and I think we both are happy about that. I certainly am. I get a lot from our friendship.'

'So if that is a valid interpretation of your dream, was God speaking to you in it?'

'Yes… well, yes … for me it feels like having God's blessing on our friendship when I think of it. And that will be there whatever happens to her physical condition. You know, I *will* tell her, and mention what I think it means for me. I'll leave it up to her to say if it means anything to her. She'll probably go away and think about if I know her, then she'll get back to me.'

'Sounds as if you've got a good friend there - and a wise one!'

[41] This story is told in the Book of Genesis, chapter 41

Why do you dream?

Scientists still have competing views on why people dream. One factor that seems to lead to great confusion is that newborn babies can spend more than half their life, not only asleep, but dreaming. Surely they are not trying to understand their lives better in the process? And then there is that undeniable fact that most dreams are so quickly and easily forgotten, that it seems almost unnatural not only try to remember, but even to try to interpret them.

It was fashionable a few years ago to say that dreams were merely the result of randomly firing sparks of electricity in the chemical circuits of the brain, and therefore, could have no meaning. The scientists who launched it have now discredited their own theory.

Perhaps while we wait for scientists to tell us the definitive reason, we have to risk thinking for ourselves and acting on our own beliefs about dreaming.

Waking up to my dreams has enriched my life. My dreams have provided me with lots of healthy laughter, and with fascinating stories and discussions to share with friends. I continue to learn from searching for their disguised wisdom, perhaps especially from feeling the discomfort and yet the security of their challenging ethical promptings. I believe my dreams help me to process what happens in my life day by day. They are one way to explore other dimensions in my understanding of myself that I experience as sometimes deeply spiritual yet often truly earthy.

What is your belief about why you dream? Your answer to that will greatly influence what you do about them. If you haven't done so already, I hope you will decide to try waking up to your dreams.

Appendix 1
A POSSIBLE STRUCTURE FOR RECORDING A DREAM

Date: Title:

Dream record:

The theme of the dream:

Context of the dream:

Emotions:

Symbols in this dream: (roughly sketch or describe any symbol difficult to interpret just now)

a) My dream body image:

b) Other people:

c) Other symbols:

Metaphors:

My interpretation:

Any action I should take:

Appendix 2.
COMPILING A PERSONAL DREAM DICTIONARY

Preparing to start

Dictionaries are usually compiled in alphabetical order. A computer will arrange them alphabetically for you, but if you choose to write instead find a large format address book with pages for each letter of the alphabet, or have a loose-leaf folder with cardboard dividers.

You will be handling a variety of dream symbols

Have them all in one list, or try having separate sections for different kinds of dream symbols.

a) People

- People you know will appear as symbols in your dreams. List them.

- You will also meet people you can't identify by name. Identify them in some other way: e.g. 'A presence with me, probably male. Felt supported.' Or 'blonde woman in purple slacks. Felt uneasy with her

there.' 'A group of people: looked like tourists'

- I enjoy having a separate list for my dreaming self-image. Usually it'll be a 'just me' image, but if not, I suggest you note your apparent age, gender, dress, ethnic origin, anything unusual about your dream body, what you were doing, thinking, feeling …

b) Symbols of things that are of special interest to you

Some people name locations in their dreams - cities, rivers, countries, while others note makes of cars, types of transport, food, colours. Probably depends on your particular interests in your waking life. If you have a speciality like these, you might choose to have a separate section in your dictionary for its symbols.

c) Mysterious symbols

Sooner or later you'll come across a mystery object in your dream that you can't identify. Draw it, or describe it as fully as you can. Once you discover its meaning for you, you might find a name for it, and file it alphabetically. I keep my drawings.

d) Activities

Build up a list of actions you can readily interpret when they occur - dancing, flying, feeling trapped, jumping off high walls, falling, wandering…

e) Symbols with similar meanings

Another way to group symbols is by what they mean for you. Gather under separate headings symbols of things (including people) that give you security, pleasure, worry, fear, and so on.

Symbolic significance

The importance of all these symbols is that they have a particular significance for you. Beside each, write your interpretation of why they have come into your dreaming.

Why make a personal dream symbol dictionary?

Compiling a personal dream dictionary honours your own experience, your personal history that has helped and continues to help you make meaning in your life. Making such a dictionary takes time, but sometimes it saves time in the long run. It can give you personal short-cuts in interpretation, taking you over familiar ground.

Symbols sometimes change in their significance for you

Each time a specific symbol occurs you might discover that you give it exactly the same meaning, or you might want to place a second or even a third meaning under the first entry. If they change, ask yourself why.

And symbols themselves sometimes change

Your dream presents you with a familiar symbol, but there's something different about it. It has changed colour, or shape, or size. Sometimes something has happened to it - it has crumbled, or been placed in a new situation.

You'll probably find the same symbols occur in your dreams time and again. They reflect the way your mind manages your life.

Your symbols carry your meaning

A dream dictionary can become an emotional health checklist for you, but don't impose your familiarity with your meanings on other dreamers' symbols!

Some examples

Here are a few fictitious examples. You don't
need to standardise your style.

- Aunt Liz: The pioneer spirit in our
  family

- Uncle John: Apparently he's still
  putting a damper on things for me!

- My car: I'm driving. I feel in control.

- Taking a taxi: I had to supply
  directions.

- Jumping off a high wall: I was taking
  a risk. I landed safely.

- Yellow: Sheer happiness.

Enjoy this journey of discovery into
your own mind and heart!

BIBLIOGRAPHY

Aserinsky, Eugene and Kleitman, Nathaniel (1953): 'Regular periods of eye motility and concomitant phenomena during sleep'. *Science 118*: 273, 4.

Barnes, Colin; Mercer, Geoff; Shakespeare, Tom (Eds., reprinted 2000): *Exploring Disability: A Sociological Introduction*. London, Blackwell.

Cusk, Rachel (1997): *The Country Life.* London, Macmillan.

Dement, William C. (2001): *The Promise of Sleep*. London, Pan.

Federn, Paul (1953): *Ego Psychology and the Psychoses*. New York, Basic Books.

Fontana, David (1999): *Dreams: An Introductory Guide to Unlocking the Secrets of Your Dream Life.* Longmead, Dorset. Element Books.

Freud, Sigmund (1999): *The Interpretation of Dreams. A new translation by Joyce Crick.* Oxford, Oxford University Press. (Original work published 1899).

Gallese, Vittoria & Goldman, Alvin (1998): 'Mirror neurons and the simulation theory of mind-reading'. *Trends in Cognitive Sciences* 2.12.

Greenfield, Susan (1997): *The Human Brain. A guided tour.* London, Weidenfield & Nicolson.

Hartmann, Ernest (1996): 'Who Develops PTSD Nightmares and Who Doesn't?' In Barrett, Deirdre (ed.) *Trauma and Dreams* pp.100-113, Cambridge, Massachusetts, Harvard University Press.

Head, Henry (1920): *Studies in Neurology, Vol.2.* London, Hodder and Stoughton and Oxford University Press.

Hobson, J., Pace-Schott, E. & Stickgold, R. (2000): 'Dreaming and the Brain : Towards a Cognitive Neuroscience of Conscious States', *Behavioral and Brain Sciences*, 23(6).

Hurovitz, Craig S., Dunn, Sarah, Domhoff, G. W. and Fiss, H. (1999): 'The Dreams of Blind Men and Women: A Replication and Extension of Previous Findings'. *Dreaming 9, 2 - 3.*

Jung, C.J. (1967): *Memories, Dreams, Reflections*. London, Collins Fontana.

Kaplan-Solms, Karen and Solms, Mark (2000): *Clinical Studies in Neuro-Psychoanalysis. Introduction to a Depth Neuropsychology.* London, Karnac Books.

Kerr, N. (1993): 'Mental imagery, dreams, and perception'. In D. Foulkes and C. Cavallero (Eds.), *Dreaming as Cognition* (pp.18 - 37). New York, Harvester Wheatsheaf.

Kolb, L. (1959): 'Disturbance of Body Image'. *American Handbook of Psychiatry, Vol. 1, Chapter 38*. New York, Basic Books.

Lowy, S.(1942): *Foundations of Dream Interpretation.* Kegan Paul, Trench and Trubner.

Matlock, T. (1988): 'The metaphorical extensions of "see"'. In J. Emonds et al. (Ed.), *Proceedings of the Western Conference on Linguistics.*

Matlock, T., and Sweetser, E. (1989): *Semantic change of perception verbs to evidentials and mental state verbs.* Unpublished manuscript. University of California, Santa Cruz.

Mead, Juliette (2003): *Healing Flynn.* London, HarperCollins Publishers.

Melbourne, David, F. & Hearne, Keith (1999): *The Meaning of Your Dreams: An Interactive Guide.* London, Blandford.

Ramachandran, V.S. & Blakeslee, S. (1999): *Phantoms in the Brain.* New York, William Morrow.

Ryan, James H. (1961): 'Dreams of Paraplegics'. *Archives of General Psychiatry 5.* 286 - 291.

Solms, Mark (1997): *The Neuropsychology of Dreams.* Mahwah New Jersey, Lawrence Earlbaum Associates.

Solms, Mark and Turnbull, Oliver (2002): *The Brain and the Inner World.* New York, Other Press.

Swain, John; French, Sally; & Cameron, Colin (Eds., 2003): *Controversial Issues in a Disabling Society,* Open University Press.

Sweetser, E. (1990): *From Etymology to Pragmatics.* New York, Cambridge University Press.

Vollmar, Klaus (1997): *The Little Giant Encyclopaedia of Dream Symbols.* New York, Sterling Publishing Company.

Wunder, Delores F. (1993): 'Dreams as Empirical Data: Siblings' Dreams and Fantasies About Their Disabled Sisters and Brothers'. *Symbolic Interaction*, 16.2: 117 - 127.

ABOUT THE AUTHOR

 Born and brought up near Glasgow, Jean Morrison worked first as a school teacher then as a parish deaconess in Castlemilk. She studied adult education and pastoral psychology for a year in Chicago and California, and for three years trained youth workers in Australia, before coming home to take up a national appointment in the Church of Scotland, and marry Bill. With her husband she fostered teenagers before returning to employment as the first Director of the Pastoral Foundation in Edinburgh. Since 1993 she has been a counsellor, supervisor and trainer in private practice, and during that time became a Doctor in Psychotherapy through Professional Studies. This book on dreaming is a product of her research.